Being Catholic in a Culture of Choice

Being Catholic in a Culture of Choice

Thomas P. Rausch, S.J.

A Michael Glazier Book

LITURGICAL PRESS
Collegeville, Minnesota

www.litpress.org

A Michael Glazier Book published by Liturgical Press.

Cover design by Ann Blattner. Photo by Greg Becker.

Library of Congress Cataloging-in-Publication Data

Rausch, Thomas P.
　　Being Catholic in a culture of choice / Thomas P. Rausch.
　　　　p.　cm.
　　"A Michael Glazier book."
　　Includes index.
　　ISBN-13:　978-0-8146-5984-7
　　ISBN-10:　0-8146-5984-5
　1. Catholic Church.　I. Title.

　BX1754.R38　2006
　282—dc22

2006014461

Eugene R. Growney, S.J.

In memoriam

Contents

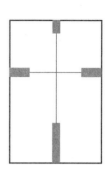

Acknowledgments   ix

Introduction   xi
   Characteristics of Catholic Identity   xii
   Diverse Perspectives   xv

CHAPTER 1
Young Adult Catholics   1
   The Research   3
   A Diminished Catholic Identity   4
   Contributing Factors   9
   Conclusion   18

CHAPTER 2
The Catholic Imagination   20
   Approaching the Ultimate   23
   Roots of the Catholic Imagination   24
   Catholic and Protestant Expressions   27
   Conclusion   35

CHAPTER 3
The Catholic Tradition and *The Da Vinci Code*   36
   Questionable Sources   37
   The Church's Struggle with Gnosticism   39
   Jesus and Mary Magdalene   45
   Other Errors   47
   Conclusion   49

CHAPTER 4
The Domestic Church   51

Handing on the Faith   52

The Church in the Home   53

Expressions of the Domestic Church   57

Conclusion   64

CHAPTER 5
Catholic Colleges and Universities   66

The Process of Professionalization   67

Ex Corde Ecclesiae   69

Theology and Religious Studies   71

Preserving Catholic Identity   75

Conclusion   85

CHAPTER 6
A New Generation?   87

Evangelical Catholics   89

Seminarians   91

Younger Catholic Theologians   96

Converts and Reverts   99

Conclusion   100

CHAPTER 7
Some Concluding Reflections   102

Spiritual but not Religious   102

Authority in a Church of Choice   105

Catholic Identity and the New Apologists   109

The Uniqueness of Catholicism   111

Conclusion   114

Index   120

Acknowledgments

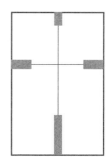

The basic inspiration for this book came from a College Theology Society panel in June, 2005 on William Portier's paper, "Here Come the Evangelical Catholics."[1] Though I drew on a number of surveys, much of its research and its subtitle come from the work of Dean R. Hoge and his associates, *Young Adult Catholics: Religion in the Culture of Choice.*[2] Part of Chapter 6 appeared in *America* magazine in October 2002 under the title, "Another Generation Gap." I'm grateful to Susan Sink of Fullerton College, Fullerton, California, who did the copyediting and to our graduate assistant, Deb Pavelek, for her careful proofreading and suggestions.

Catholic identity is a many faceted issue. While the profile emerging from various surveys of young Catholics raises some serious questions about how the Church hands on its tradition and incorporates young people into its life, I want to express my admiration for the many young people I've met in my years of teaching. I have learned much from them, and appreciate the many gifts they bring to the Church.

Thomas P. Rausch, S.J.

[1] William L. Portier, "Here Come the Evangelical Catholics," *Communio* 31 (Spring 2004) 35–66.

[2] Dean R. Hoge, William D. Dinges, Mary Johnson, and Juan L. Gonzales, Jr., *Young Adult Catholics: Religion in the Culture of Choice* (Notre Dame, IN: University of Notre Dame Press, 2001).

Introduction

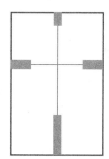

What will the next generation of Catholics be like? Will they have a strong sense of their Catholic identity, or will they reflect a more generic Christian identity, without the distinctives associated with Catholicism? A number of social commentators such as Dean R. Hoge and James J. Davidson and their associates suggest that the Catholic identity of young Catholics is in jeopardy.[1] Others today argue that there are signs that a new generation of younger Catholics is emerging, not all of whom fall easily into the liberal/conservative categories, though many Catholics over fifty tend to dismiss them as conservative, neoconservative, or even restorationist.

Catholic identity is an issue not only for young adults. Catholics of all ages are grappling with how to preserve a sense of who they are. In a predominantly secular, postmodern culture—Hoge calls it a "culture of choice"—many people are constructing their own religious identities.[2] Religious affiliation or church membership is strictly voluntary, to be chosen on the basis of personal preference.

Furthermore, many younger Catholics are quite unfamiliar with their religious tradition. The Scriptures are a mystery to them, they know little of the history or doctrine of their church, and few would be able to tell the stories of the saints.

---

[1] James D. Davidson and Dean R. Hoge, "Catholics After the Scandal: A New Study's Major Findings," *Commonweal* 131/20 (November 19, 2004) 13–18.

[2] Dean R. Hoge, William D. Dinges, Mary Johnson, Juan L. Gonzales, Jr., *Young Adult Catholics: Religion in the Culture of Choice* (Notre Dame, IN: University of Notre Dame Press, 2001).

So what are the characteristics of a Catholic identity? What are its root metaphors, its interpretative impulses? How and where does it encounter the divine?

Characteristics of Catholic Identity

Before looking at what Catholics believe, it is important to understand how they experience the world and God. In his book, *Catholicism*, Richard McBrien identifies two characteristic foci of the Catholic tradition—one philosophical, the other theological.[3]

The philosophical focus is Christian realism. Realism means that knowledge begins from experience, but moves beyond it. Catholic thought recognizes that critical reason can pierce the phenomenal veil and grasp, however imperfectly, the mystery of the absolute implied in its questioning and its knowing. It also knows that God has first addressed us with the divine word, mediated by the Hebrew Scriptures, proclaimed by the prophets, and ultimately incarnated in the Word become flesh. If sacred Scripture witnesses to God's self-disclosure in human history and experience, it is still the word of God in the words of human beings, and so must be interpreted in a way that honors both its human modalities of expression and the divine initiative that lies behind it.

Because of the inclusive nature of Catholicism, it is not bound to a single philosophy, theology, or theological school, but is able to draw on and utilize many approaches and methods. Catholicism is pluralistic in its approach to truth. At the same time, there is a distinctively Catholic way of integrating the pluralism of philosophies and theologies in the search for the truth.

Catholicism rejects both idealism and naïve realism, along with the latter's offspring, empiricism and biblical fundamentalism. Human beings discover meaning through experience, but also through critical questioning, historical investigation, systematizing ideas, and asking further questions. Knowledge is more than taking a look. Like the operation of the intellect itself, the knower must return always to the concrete, the experiential, and the observable. This is true even in the realm of faith. Even if faith is a gift and calls for trust, reason and faith must work in consort.

[3] Richard P. McBrien, *Catholicism* (HarperSanFrancisco, 1994) 1192–1200.

McBrien also points to three theological foci of Catholicism: sacramentality, mediation, and communion. Sacramentality refers to the sense for the disclosure of the divine mystery through a nature damaged but still graced. God is not distant, so transcendent as to be beyond our reach, but reflected in the beauty of nature, intuited in human love, grasped in the experience of community.

Mediation stresses that grace, God's invisible presence, is always disclosed or experienced through some concrete symbol or event, first of all in the man Jesus, then through other signs and instruments of salvation, natural, scriptural, and ecclesial. As Louis-Marie Chauvet says, "Reality is never present to us except in a mediated way, which is to say, constructed out of the symbolic network of the culture which fashions us."[4]

The encounter with God is always a mediated experience. In the Catholic tradition, grace is mediated in a special way by the sacraments; they both symbolize and cause. Baptism symbolizes new life in Christ and mediates it by initiating the one baptized into a community where Christ is proclaimed, praised, and celebrated by those living in his Spirit. Penance proclaims God's forgiveness and reconciliation to those who seek it in Jesus' name. Marriage celebrates and makes real God's unconditional love and Christ's union with his people in the love of husband and wife for each other and for the children born of their love.

In traditional Catholic language, grace builds on nature. Unlike Reformation theology, Catholicism takes a "both-and" approach; not Scripture alone, but Scripture and tradition; not faith alone, but faith and works as well as faith and reason; not grace alone, but grace and nature.

Communion recognizes that our way to God is communal. God deals with us as a people and touches us through others; one cannot be a Christian alone. Mediation is always made possible by the community, for Catholicism recognizes the radically social nature of the human person. Catholicism is nervous about a religious individualism that reduces the life of grace to a "personal relationship" with Jesus, without reference to the mediating and challenging role of the community. Our relationship to God cannot be separated from our relationships to other human beings; we cannot be "saved" all by ourselves. The Church is a pilgrim people; we are always "on the way."

[4] Louis-Marie Chauvet, *Symbol and Sacrament: A Sacramental Reinterpretation of Christian Existence,* trans. Patrick Madigan and Madeleine Beaumont (Collegeville, MN: Liturgical Press, 1995) 41.

Andrew Greeley says that sacramentality, community, and hierarchy distinguish Catholicism.[5] Acknowledging the work of David Tracy, he sees the distinctive experience of Catholics as rooted in their Catholic or "sacramental" imagination. "Catholics," he writes, "live in an enchanted world, a world of statues and holy water, stained glass and votive candles, saints and religious medals, rosary beads and holy pictures," which are for him only hints of a much deeper religious sensitivity to the divine presence lurking in created reality, in nature, stories, human loves, and religious symbols.[6] The sacramental imagination prizes art and the symbolic, it emphasizes community, and recognizes the place of hierarchy. We will explore Greeley's sacramental imagination and consider its theological roots in a further chapter.

Catholicism as an Ecclesial Faith

For Catholic Christians, the Church is always more than a community formed in response to the word, a voluntary assembly of the faithful, or a visible religious institution; the Church mediates God's saving presence through its Scriptures, its tradition, its preaching, teaching, ministry, worship, and fellowship. Catholicism is an essentially ecclesial faith.

Catholic identity traditionally has included for Catholics a sense for the historical uniqueness of their Church; they understand it as a world-wide, visible community, now almost two thousand years old, with roots stretching back to the church of the apostles. They have a reverence for its hierarchical ministry, its papal-episcopal teaching authority, and its tradition. That tradition includes sacramentality, a strong liturgical tradition centered on the Eucharist, an incarnational theology, a lively sense for the communion of the saints with a special veneration of Mary the "mother of God," a rich tradition of spirituality, mysticism, and contemplative prayer. Catholics honor monasticism and the religious life, have a sense for the complementarity of faith and reason, and a deep appreciation of the religious value of art. They have a strong sense for community, including a communal understanding of sin and salvation and a highly developed social teaching based on the dignity of the human

---

[5] Andrew M. Greeley, *The Catholic Imagination* (Berkeley: University of California Press, 2000) 137.

[6] Ibid., 1; cf. David Tracy, *The Analogical Imagination: Christian Theology and the Culture of Pluralism* (New York: Crossroad, 1986).

person and the principle of the common good.[7] Solidarity is a key concept.

We might summarize these attempts to delineate a Catholic identity by pointing to an ecclesial faith, a visible, hierarchical church, a sacramental imagination, a theology that seeks to integrate both faith and reason, and a strong communal sense.

Diverse Perspectives

We will explore the question of Catholic identity today from a number of different perspectives. Chapter 1 reviews a number of recent studies on young Catholics. Focusing on their religious individualism, these studies call attention to their less ecclesial faith, their "thin" commitment to the institutional church, their tendency to construct their own religious identities, and their lack of familiarity with the stories, root metaphors, and doctrines of their tradition. While some no longer practice their faith or have "left" the Church, there is also a smaller group of young people strongly committed to the Church.

Drawing on the work of Greeley, Chapter 2 studies the Catholic sacramental imagination, contrasting the way Catholics and Protestants experience the holy as well as the theological insights and religious anthropologies that underlie and support their respective religious imaginations.

Chapter 3 looks at Dan Brown's enormously popular book, *The Da Vinci Code*. Reviewing the book's charges against the Catholic Church brings to light the Church's formative role in shaping the Christian tradition, particularly in its biblical and theological expressions. Given the pluralism of contemporary Christianity and the general ignorance of Christian origins, recovering an informed sense for that role is essential to an adult Catholic identity.

Chapter 4 examines the "domestic church," the Christian family that plays such an important role in developing the religious identity and experience of those who grow up in Christian homes. For Catholics that identity is mediated through story and symbol, prayer, ritual, and sacrament, with the family itself as the primary sacramental experience.

---

[7] Thomas P. Rausch, *Catholicism in the Third Millennium,* Second Edition (Collegeville, MN: Liturgical Press, 2003) xii–xiv.

Chapter 5 turns to Catholic colleges and universities, institutions of higher learning where the Church does its thinking and future generations of Catholics are given the opportunity to become familiar with the rich heritage of their faith. Originally institutions created by the Church to bring an immigrant Catholic population into the mainstream, today those institutions, aware of the loss of religious identity of so many originally Protestant schools, are caught up in a struggle to preserve and enhance their Catholic identity in the predominantly secular, postmodernist culture of the academy.

Chapter 6 turns to a significant and growing minority of young Catholics who are passionate about their faith and enthusiastic in their identity as Catholic Christians. While some of the Vatican II generation are too quick to dismiss this group as neoconservative, restorationist, or sectarian, for a number of reasons such designations are too facile. The defining moments in their young lives are simply different from those a generation or two ahead of them. With so many seminarians, religious, and theologians among them, many see them as moving into leadership positions in tomorrow's Church.

Chapter 7 offers some concluding reflections on a number of issues considered earlier, among them spirituality, authority in the Church, the new apologists, and the uniqueness of the Catholic Church, exploring them at a greater depth.

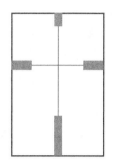

Chapter 1

Young Adult Catholics

How often have we heard people say, "I'm spiritual but not religious"? This often remarked upon disconnecting of spirituality from religion means, in effect, that more and more Americans are choosing their own religious identity.

A new study on the spiritual life of college students by UCLA's Higher Education Research Institute surveyed 3,680 undergraduates from 46 diverse colleges and universities. The study's findings were optimistic, reporting a high level of spiritual engagement and commitment among college students. Seventy-seven percent of students said "we are all spiritual beings," and 71 percent reported that they "gain spiritual strength by trusting in a higher power." Among third-year students, three in four reported that they prayed, discussed religion and spirituality with friends, and found religion personally helpful. Some 86 percent of those surveyed listed attaining wisdom as an "essential" or "very important" goal in life. However the "ultimate spiritual quest" most often selected included "to become a better person" (30 percent), "to know what God requires of me" (14 percent), and "to know my purpose in life" (13 percent).

At the same time, most of the respondents acknowledged a decline in religious practice during their college years. More than half (52 percent) reported attending religious services frequently before entering college, but by their junior year less than one-third (29 percent) attended frequently; only 9 percent said that their spirituality had become stronger.[1]

In 2004 the survey was expanded to first-year students at 236 institutions. Again the students reported high levels of spiritual interest and

[1] See www.spirituality.ucla.edu.

involvement. Interestingly, in this survey the highest percentage of entering freshmen was Catholic (28 percent), followed by mainline Protestants (17 percent), Baptists (13 percent), and "other Christians" (11 percent). Catholic respondents tended to score *below* the overall average on religious commitment, religious engagement, religious/social conservatism, and religious skepticism (the last being unusual, since those who score low on the first three standards usually score high on religious skepticism).

The discrepancy between the optimistic charting of spiritual interest and the low level of religious practice or spiritual growth leads one to wonder if the researchers may have defined spirituality too broadly, even uncritically. Many social scientists tend to write as though religion and spirituality are mutually exclusive. Religion is narrowly described as formal and institutional, while spirituality is seen as personal and experiential.[2]

The UCLA researchers sought to assess student spirituality and religiousness on the basis of twelve "scales," spirituality, being on a spiritual quest, equanimity, charitable involvement, compassionate self-concept, an ethic of caring, and an ecumenical worldview as well as five indicators of student religiousness: religious commitment, engagement, skepticism, struggle, and religious/social conservatism. Missing was any real effort to survey "practice" such as ascetic discipline, bodily exercise, regular prayer or meditation, journaling, spiritual direction, or service that traditionally have been considered signs of a genuine spirituality.[3] But if the concept of spirituality in the UCLA survey seems "fuzzy," to use Zillbauer and Pargament's term,[4] it may well be that the concept of spirituality shared by many young adults is equally fuzzy.

One of our concerns in this book is the religious identity of young adult Catholics. While there are different ways of measuring who count as young adults, I apply the term to those between the ages of 20 and 39, a group that constitutes about 40 percent of the U.S. Catholic population.

---

[2] For example, Brian Zillbauer and Kenneth Pargament et al., "Religion and Spirituality: Unfuzzying the Fuzzy," *The Journal for the Scientific Study of Religion,* 36/4 (1997) 549–84; Penny Long Marler and C. Kirk Hadaway, "'Being Religious' or 'Being Spiritual': in America: A Zero-Sum Proposition?" *The Journal for the Scientific Study of Religion* 41/2 (2002) 289–300.

[3] Cf. John A. Coleman, "Social Science and Spirituality," *The Blackwell Companion to Christian Spirituality,* ed. Arthur Holder (Malden, MA: Basil Blackwell, 2005) 289–307.

[4] Cf. Zillbauer and Pargament, "Religion and Spirituality: Unfuzzying the Fuzzy."

The description that follows generalizes trends as measured by surveys; it does not describe *all* those in this particular group. In addition to the UCLA study which is still in process, we will draw on a number of recent studies and surveys.

The Research

1. *The Search for Common Ground (Davidson 1997)*

James J. Davidson and his associates, in a national telephone poll, surveyed Catholics in 49 parishes in five Indiana dioceses. Their research appeared in 1997 under the title, *The Search for Common Ground: What Unites and Divides Catholic Americans.*[5] It identified young Catholics as "post–Vatican II Catholics."

2. *Young Adult Catholics (Hoge 2001)*

Another significant study specifically on young adult Catholics is Dean R. Hoge and his colleagues' work, *Young Adult Catholics: Religion in the Culture of Choice.* The study represents research done in 1997 on a sample of the twenty million young adult Catholics between 20 and 39 years of age, roughly 40 percent of the Catholic population.[6] The researchers telephoned confirmands in 44 parishes in 11 dioceses throughout the nation. They also made a separate sample of Latinos. Because the research focused on young adult Catholics, it will be our basic source.

3. *Notre Dame Study (Notre Dame 2004)*

In 2002 the University of Notre Dame established a task force to survey the laity on issues facing the Church, with a special emphasis on generational differences. To identify these differences, the researchers identified four generations: pre–Vatican II Catholics (born in or before 1940), Vatican II Catholics, (born 1941–1960); post–Vatican II Catholics (born 1961–1977), and millennial Catholics (born 1978–1985). The researchers interviewed

[5] Davidson, et al., *The Search for Common Ground: What Unites and Divides Catholic Americans* (Huntington, IN: Our Sunday Visitor, 1997).

[6] Dean R. Hoge, William D. Dinges, Mary Johnson, Juan L. Gonzales, Jr., *Young Adult Catholics: Religion in the Culture of Choice* (Notre Dame, IN: University of Notre Dame Press, 2001) 3.

a random sample of 1,119 self-identified Catholics. The results were published in 2004.[7]

4. *National Catholic Reporter Survey (NCR 2005)*

Another useful instrument is an 18-year survey of Catholic attitudes and commitment, undertaken by Davidson, Hoge, William V. D'Antonio, and Mary Gautier at the suggestion of the *National Catholic Reporter (NCR)*. The most recent results of this survey were published in 2005. It divides post–Vatican II Catholics—half of all Catholics today—into three groups: post–Vatican II Catholics (born 1941–1960), Generation X Catholics (1961–1978), and millennials (1979–1987).[8]

5. *University of North Carolina Study (UNC 2005)*

Finally, we will draw on a wide study of youth and religion conducted by researchers at the University of North Carolina at Chapel Hill and published in 2005.[9] The study focused on teenagers between the ages of 13 and 17. Some 3,370 teenagers and one of their parents were surveyed, and an additional 267 in-depth interviews were conducted through randomly generated telephone numbers, making this an extremely useful instrument.

A Diminished Catholic Identity

How might the religious identity of young adult Catholics in the United States be characterized today? Many have observed that they share the subjective approach of their non-Catholic peers toward religious affiliation. The bonds that tie them to the institutional Church have slipped considerably. Richard Gaillardetz reports that from his experience of speaking at dozens of pastoral events over the last 15 years, two issues surface repeatedly.

---

[7] Davidson and Hoge, "Catholics After the Scandal: A New Study's Major Findings," *Commonweal* 131/20 (Nov. 19, 2004) 13–19.

[8] See "Survey of U.S. Catholics," *National Catholic Reporter* 41/42 (September 30, 2005) 9–24; also ncronline.org/NCR_Online/archives2/2005d/101405/101405n. htm.

[9] Christian Smith and Melinda Lundquist Denton, *Soul Searching: The Religious and Spiritual Lives of American Teenagers* (New York: Oxford University Press, 2005).

1. the large numbers of young Catholics who have only a very thin sense of their Catholic identity and

2. a small but significant percentage of Catholics who seem, to the outside observer, obsessed with their Catholic identity and seek to define it in ways that alienate many pastoral ministers.[10]

Gaillardetz identifies the two different groups we noted in the Introduction, a larger group with a diminished sense of Catholic identity, and a smaller but significant group vitally interested in what it means to be Catholic.

Perhaps even more disturbing is the UNC study. The researchers found that U.S. Catholic teenagers are *behind* their Protestant peers—sometimes by as much as 25 percentage points—when measured by many standards of religious belief, practice, experiences, and commitments. Indeed, many of them are "living far outside of official Church norms defining true Catholic faithfulness."[11]

Only 10 percent of Catholic teenagers said religion was "extremely important" in shaping their daily lives, compared to 20 percent of mainline Protestants, 29 percent of conservative Protestants, and 31 percent of black Protestant teens. Forty percent of Catholic teens said that they had never attended any parish religious education programs, versus 19 percent of mainline, 13 percent of conservative, and 12 percent of black Protestants. In terms of attending religious services, 40 percent of Catholic teens attended once a week—slightly below mainline and black Protestant teens, but 15 percent lower than conservative Protestant teens. Only 6 percent of Catholic teens said they attended religious services more than once a week.[12]

A Diminished Institutional Identity

Hoge and his associates described young adult Catholics as comfortable with the Church's basic doctrines, sacramental tradition, and concern for the poor. At the same time these young Catholics lack a strong commitment to the Church and are less familiar with the ecclesial dimensions

---

[10] Richard Gaillardetz, "Apologetics, Evangelization and Ecumenism Today," *Origins* 35/1 (2005) 9.

[11] Smith and Denton, *Soul Searching*, 194.

[12] Ibid., 37–53.

of their faith.[13] The gap between what the Church teaches and what Catholics actually believe and do, the researchers noted, revealed that "a more serious issue is the decline in the centrality of Catholic institutional identity. That is, it matters less to large numbers of young adult Catholics if they are Catholic in any institutional or communal sense."[14] Indeed a significant number no longer see the Catholic Church as unique, the pope as necessary, or the tradition as a source of objective truth (221). Many said that they can be good Catholics without going to Mass (224).

The *NCR* survey bears this out, reporting that 76 percent of Catholics think that you can be a good Catholic without going to church every Sunday (Table 1); for Generation X and millennials, the percentages are even higher—76 and 95 percent respectively (Table 3). Only 26 percent of the post–Vatican II sample and 15 percent of the millennials reported attending Mass weekly or more (Table 10). A report from the Center for Applied Research in the Apostolate in Washington (CARA) notes that only 21 percent of young adults attend Mass every week or more.[15]

While Hoge et al., found that young adult Catholics like being Catholic, their Catholicism seems to be accidental to their relationship with Christ. The largest group in their sample consisted of young adults "all but indistinguishable from mainline Protestants." Many viewed the Church simply as another denomination or human institution. They considered being a Catholic an accident of birth or a personal preference, and viewed other churches as equally legitimate (223). They saw little connection between religion and spirituality (224). Few participated in small faith communities in their parishes and their social networks weren't primarily Catholic (228). In other words, being Catholic was not expressed by being part of the Catholic community. The communal dimension of Catholicism, noted earlier as a distinctive of Catholic identity, was largely missing.

A Selective Approach to Authority

Another problem is that the Church itself has little authority for many young adult Catholics. They are "less convinced that the Church's rules are God's rules, less convinced that the Church's structures are divinely

---

[13] Hoge, *Young Adult Catholics,* 220–21.

[14] Ibid., 223; see chapter 2 for a review of past research.

[15] Bryan T. Froehle and Mary L. Gautier, *Catholicism USA: A Portrait of the Catholic Church in the United States* (Maryknoll, NY: Orbis, 2000) 23.

ordained or necessary, and more inclined to make choices for themselves" (225). They are selective in their approach to Church teachings; what is true is what is true for the individual (223). The Church has little credibility in the area of sexuality; those interviewed repeatedly mentioned birth control, homosexuality, limitations on women's role in the Church, and teachings against married and women priests as the most problematic (231). The *NCR* survey said that 59 percent of post–Vatican II Catholics and 89 percent of millennials agreed that one can be a good Catholic without accepting the Church's opposition to abortion (Table 6).

Most of the undergraduates I teach have little patience with what they see as the official Church's negative attitude toward sexuality; that is, issuing black-and-white condemnations rather than articulating positive values. Many are not able to understand the Church's attitude toward homosexuals and see them as marginalized. Virtually all of them have grown up with gay friends and cannot understand why the Church cannot reevaluate its teaching in this area since it recognizes that homosexuality is a condition not a choice. They feel that homosexuals have the right to express their love physically and do not see recognizing gay marriages as undermining the institution of marriage. The refusal to support even domestic partnership seems nothing more than prejudice to them.

For many young adult Catholics, being religious is reduced to ethics. Although they consider social justice central to being Catholic, their sense of social justice has little to do with the Church's social teaching. "While they see social justice as core to Catholic identity, most individuals interpret this to mean approaching social problems with acts of charity." Being religious means simply being a good person. If they saw more clearly the connection between social justice and a *specifically Catholic identity*, including its social doctrine, they might be more concerned with structural problems, institutions, and power, the Hoge report argued. (224).

Leaving the Catholic Church?

A final example of a decreased institutional loyalty is the diminishing number of Catholics who say that they would never leave the Church. Hoge's *Young Adult Catholics* was optimistic on this issue. He said that of those his researchers interviewed, most have remained Catholic, including the Latinos. Of the 6 percent of non-Latinos and 8 percent of Latinos interviewed who had formally joined other churches, half of the

Latino sample had returned to the Catholic Church.[16] Reviewing their research, Peter Steinfels judges it to be "slightly rosier than the reality" because interviews were conducted only with those who had been confirmed. He notes that because only about 60–70 percent of non-Latino youth and 30–40 percent of Latinos were confirmed during the 1980s and 1990s, "the young adults of this study do not represent all current young adult Catholics."[17]

In the Notre Dame study of generational differences among Catholics, 81 percent said that the Catholic Church is "very important to me personally" and 71 percent said that they would never leave the Catholic Church.[18] But the *NCR* survey showed a considerable drop in those who said they would never leave: 69 percent of pre–Vatican II Catholics, 58 percent of Vatican II Catholics, 53 percent of those in Generation X and only 33 percent of the millennials (Table 3). And the number of committed Catholics steadily continues to decline. Hoge said of the *NCR* results, "Nobody should conclude that in 20 or 40 years, no Catholics will be in the high-commitment category, since church involvement typically increases from the young adult years to the middle adult years. The most reasonable prediction is that in the future the overall level will continue to sag, as it has recently."[19]

Today there are many who have left the Catholic Church and joined other churches. This is something relatively new. We once said, "Once a Catholic, always a Catholic." Not so any more. The reasons people leave are many. Some, the object of proselytizing efforts by evangelical Christians, claim to have discovered a personal relationship with Jesus for the first time. Some of the seeker megachurches such as Willow Creek near Chicago, claim to have more than 60 percent former Catholics among their ranks. A significant number of Hispanic Catholics have joined evangelical churches, too.

Some Catholics have left after running afoul of the Church's discipline or because of impatience with what they saw as the Church's inability to change, particularly in its teaching against married and women priests. I've met a number of Catholics who left because of abuses of Church authority. In one case, a woman whose book on preaching had been accepted by a Catholic press was told by a priest that she could not say

---

[16] Hoge, *Young Adult Catholics*, 44–46.

[17] Peter Steinfels, *A People Adrift* (New York: Simon and Schuster, 2003) 209.

[18] Davidson and Hoge, "Catholics After the Scandal," 17–18.

[19] Hoge, "Attitudes of Catholics Highly Committed to the Church," *NCR* Survey.

"when we preach" because she was a layperson and, therefore, not allowed to preach (he wasn't completely accurate).

Others who leave are Catholics in second marriages. Or, perhaps they married a non-Catholic and joined a Protestant church. Some leave for seemingly frivolous reasons, such as not being allowed to hold their marriage ceremony in a garden.

Many Protestant seminaries or divinity schools have large numbers of former Catholics, particularly Catholic women, who are seeking ordination. In California at least two Episcopalian bishops are former Catholics, and of the Catholic students or colleagues I've known in my years teaching in Los Angeles, at least five have become Episcopalian priests.

Contributing Factors

What contributes to this diminished sense of Catholic identity? Drawing on the Hoge study and other authors, we can point to a number of factors.

Religious Individualism

The pervasive religious individualism of postmodern American culture has often been noted. Robert Neelly Bellah attributes it to the dominance of Protestantism in the national culture of the United States, citing G. K. Chesterton's remark that "in America, even the Catholics are Protestant."[20] Bellah sees a connection between Protestantism and the utilitarian and expressive individualism so characteristic of the American cultural code. One cause of this was the role played in early American history by dissenting Protestants—sectarians persecuted by established churches in the old country who consequently exalted freedom of conscience against any political, hierocratic, or patriarchal power. As a result, the individual conscience, unbalanced by any sense for the whole or the common good, became absolutely sacred in matters of belief.

In addition, certain central Protestant beliefs strengthened that individualism. First, Bellah argues that Protestant suspicion of the Catholic

[20] Robert Neelly Bellah, "Religion and the Shape of National Culture," *America* 181/3 (1999) 10.

sense for the sacred in the world led Calvin to so emphasize the radical transcendence of God that, in effect, God was pushed out of the world. This opened the door to an atheistic naturalism. With God absent from a deterministically conceived physical universe, the self emerged as autonomous.

Second, he points to the almost exclusive American Protestant emphasis on salvation as based on a personal relationship with Jesus. This results in the privatization of piety and a Gnostic divinization of the self. A view that "if I'm all right with Jesus, then I don't need the church," can easily progress to what he calls "Sheila-ism," a name Bellah gives to the "religion" of Sheila Larson, a young woman profiled in his *Habits of the Heart* who described her faith as "just my own little voice."[21] There lies the problem. Without mediators between the individual and his or her idea of God—mediators to which one might be answerable, whether church, sacrament, canonical discipline, or doctrinal tradition—the individual emerges as autonomous.

This radical individualism can be seen in what Robert Wuthnow describes as the breakdown of communities because of the "loose connections" and "porous institutions" typical of our culture. The result is that there is little in the way of community to hold individuals together.[22] Wade Clark Roof observes that many find their experience of the sacred outside religious institutions; their approach to religion is highly subjective, exalting experience at the expense of religious authority.[23]

Similarly, Meredith McGuire describes the "spiritual autonomy" of many contemporary believers who "feel free to choose components of their individual faith and practice, combining elements of their official religious traditions with other culturally available elements."[24] These Catholics are often called "cafeteria Catholics." Typical would be the following from Sarah Michelle Gellar, star of television's *Buffy the Vampire Slayer*: "I consider myself a spiritual person. I believe in an idea of God, although it's my own personal idea. I find most religions interesting,

---

[21] Ibid., 11–12 at 12.

[22] Robert Wuthnow, *Loose Connections: Joining Together in America's Fragmented Communities* (Cambridge, MA: Harvard University Press, 1998).

[23] Wade Clark Roof, *Spiritual Marketplace: Baby Boomers and the Remaking of Religion* (Princeton, NJ: Princeton University Press, 1999); also his *A Generation of Seekers: The Spiritual Journey of the Baby Boomer Generation* (San Francisco: HarperCollins, 1993).

[24] Meredith B. McGuire, "Mapping Contemporary American Spirituality: A Sociological Perspective," *Christian Spirituality Bulletin* 5/1 (1997) 4.

and I've been to every kind of denomination: Catholic, Christian, Jewish, Buddhist. I've taken bits from everything and customized it."[25]

Post–Vatican II Catholics are the most individualistic, according to Andrea Williams and Davidson. "Most members of this age group placed great emphasis on having a personal relationship with God and did not see the Church as an essential component of their faith."[26] This seems to be an increasing trend. Davidson said that we should expect a growing number of young adults who will have a more individualistic view of their relationship with God and attach much less importance to the institutional Church.[27]

The UNC study said that "religious languages and vocabularies of commitment, duty, faithfulness, obedience, calling, obligation, account-ability, and ties to the past are nearly completely absent from the dis-course of U.S. teenagers. Instead, religion is presumed to be something that individuals choose and must reaffirm for themselves based on their present and ongoing personal felt needs and preferences."[28]

What emerges is what the authors call "Moralistic Therapeutic Deism." They call this the de facto dominant religion among contemporary U.S. teenagers, though they suggest that it may well be "the new mainstream American religious faith for our culturally post–Christian, individualis-tic, mass-consumer capitalist society."[29] Its creed would look something like this:

1. A God exists who created and orders the world and watches over human life on earth.

2. God wants people to be good, nice, and fair to each other, as taught in the Bible and by most world religions.

3. The central goal of life is to be happy and to feel good about oneself.

4. God does not need to be particularly involved in one's life except when God is needed to resolve a problem.

5. Good people go to heaven when they die.[30]

---

[25] *Christianity Today* (July 8, 2002) 10.
[26] Andrea Williams and Davidson, "Catholic Conceptions of Faith: A Generational Analysis" *Sociology of Religion* 57/3 (Fall 1996) 285.
[27] *National Catholic Reporter* (September 30, 2005) 21.
[28] Smith and Denton, *Soul Searching*, 143–44.
[29] Ibid., 262.
[30] Ibid., 162–63.

A Culture of Voluntarism

The religious individualism typical of American culture results in a religious voluntarism. As with so many people in postmodern culture, for many young Catholics being Catholic "is less a matter of core identity and more a matter of personal choice."[31] Their religious identities are self-constructed. Drawing on "America's free-market religious economy," they seek spiritual sustenance from a diversity of sources, not all of them Catholic. They refer to popular writers such as M. Scott Peck, Joseph Campbell, Laura Schlesinger, and James Dobson as often as they do to Catholic authors such as Henri Nouwen and Thomas Merton (163). They differ from Catholics of another generation in terms of their involvement in the Church's life, their selective attitude toward authority, their tendency to reduce being religious to ethics, and their diminished familiarity with the tradition and its core narratives.

Hoge and his colleagues argue that the cognitive dissonance between what the official Church teaches and what they personally accept doesn't really create a problem for most young adults Catholics. Since they appropriate being Catholic on their own terms, they feel no obligation to leave the Church when they disagree with its teachings (226).

Furthermore, few have any desire to share their faith with others (228). As John Haughey has observed, Catholic students, in contrast to many non-Catholic Christian students, "are very slow to make faith statements or statements about a personal relationship with Christ, even though Pope John Paul II has insisted that a personal, even intimate relationship with Christ should be the aim of our programs of catechesis in the church."[32] Various explanations are offered for this Catholic reticence, including the minority status of their immigrant Catholic ancestors in a Protestant culture; a "live and let live" attitude, arising out of an acceptance of American pluralism; a distaste for the "in-your-face" evangelism of some evangelicals or sectarian Christians; or the fact that so many contemporary Catholics are unable to explain or defend their faith when challenged.[33] It is also true that few Catholic theologians give a high priority to evangelization today.

---

[31] Hoge, *Young Adult Catholics*, 224–25.

[32] See John C. Haughey, "Why Are Catholics Slow to Profess Their Faith? Churchianity and Christ-ianity," *America* 190/18 (2004) 8–9.

[33] See Martin Pabble, "Why Don't Catholics Share Their Faith," *America* 193/7 (2005) 12.

One of the surprising results of the *NCR* survey was that a higher number of pre–Vatican II Catholics—59 percent, versus 47 percent for millennial Catholics—reported that they "cannot explain faith to others" (Table 13). Still religious illiteracy appears to be rather widespread; 49 percent of Catholics agreed that they often cannot explain their faith to others.[34]

Loss of the Catholic Subculture

William Portier, professor of Catholic Studies at the University of Dayton, agrees that Catholic identity has become a key issue. But he differs with those who simply classify today's young Catholics as "post–Vatican II Catholics," thus suggesting that the council itself contributed to their diminished Catholic identity,[35] or with sociologists like Hoge and colleagues who focus more on contemporary American pluralism. Portier argues that it makes more sense to tell the story of young adult Catholics today from the perspective of the dissolution of the American Catholic subculture.[36] Similarly, Gaillardetz argues that Catholics under age 40 live in a world characterized, "not by the suffocating insularity and rigidity of immigrant Catholicism, but by the disorienting free fall of postmodern religious pluralism."[37]

The immigrant Catholic subculture was once vast and all-embracing. Those born after 1965 have little sense of how completely American Catholics were shaped by it. Charles Morris, in his marvelous book *American Catholic,* charts the way immigrant Catholics and their leaders chose the path of separatism after finding themselves in a hostile Protestant culture. Under the firm direction of their mostly Irish bishops and priests, the American Church became the most "Roman" of the national churches.[38] American Catholics, fiercely loyal to the pope and generous in supplying the Church with priests, nuns, and brothers, were often anti-intellectual. As late as the fifties, critics like Msgr. John Tracy Ellis

---

[34] James Davidson, "Challenging Assumptions About Young Catholics," *National Catholic Reporter* (September 30, 2005) 22.

[35] Davidson, *The Search for Common Ground,* Chapter 1.

[36] William L. Portier, "Here Come the Evangelical Catholics," *Communio* 31 (Spring 2004) 49–50.

[37] Gaillardetz, "Apolgetics, Evangelization and Ecumenism Today," 10.

[38] Charles R. Morris, *American Catholic: The Saints and Sinners Who Built America's Most Powerful Church* (New York: Times Books, 1997) 134.

and Thomas O'Dea were asking why American Catholic scholarship was so undistinguished.[39]

Catholic life centered on the local parish and young Catholics were insulated from the surrounding culture through a vast network of Catholic institutions, religious practices, and relationships. The system of parochial education promoted Catholicism as a complete way of life, from grade schools through colleges and universities, for the few that went that far. Most Catholics married other Catholics. They had a rich devotional life that included weekly confession, prayer, devotion to the Eucharist expressed through the Mass, novenas, and Benediction, as well as a panoply of Marian devotions.[40] In Morris' words, they "shared an outlook on the world that was definably 'American Catholic'—disciplined, rule-bound, loyal to church and country, unrebellious, but upwardly mobile and achievement-oriented."[41]

The American Catholic Church was characterized by what David O'Brien has called the "immigrant style."[42] It was certainly distinctive. As Garry Wills describes it so poignantly in his essay, "Memories of a Catholic Boyhood":

> We grew up different, there were some places we went, and others did not—into the confessional box, for instance . . . . The habits of childhood are tenacious, and Catholicism was first experienced by us as a vast set of intermeshed childhood habits—prayers offered, heads ducked in unison, crossings, chants, christenings, grace at meals; beads, altar, incense, candles; nuns in the classroom, alternately too sweet and too severe, priests garbed black on the street and brilliant at the altar; churches lit and darkened, clothed and stripped, to the rhythm of liturgical recurrences. . . . We spoke a different language from the rest of men—not only the actual Latin memorized when we learned to "serve Mass" as altar boys. We also had odd bits of Latinized English that were not part of other six year olds' vocabulary, words like "contrition" or "transubstantiation."[43]

---

[39] See John Tracy Ellis, *American Catholics and the Intellectual Life* (Chicago: Heritage Foundation, 1956); Thomas O'Dea, *American Catholic Dilemma: An Inquiry into the Intellectual Life* (New York: Sheed & Ward, 1958).

[40] See James M. O'Toole, ed., *Habits of Devotion: Catholic Religious Practice in Twentieth-Century America* (Ithica, NY: Cornell University Press, 2004).

[41] Morris, *American Catholic*, 133.

[42] David J. O'Brien, *Public Catholicism* (Maryknoll, NY: Orbis, 1996) xi.

[43] Garry Wills, *Bare Ruined Choirs: Doubt, Prophecy, and Radical Religion* (Garden City, New York: Doubleday, 1972) 15–16.

It was only after the Second World War, when thousands of returning Catholic veterans used the GI Bill to gain a university education that the largely blue-collar Catholic population began to enter the mainstream. No longer a socially excluded minority, Catholics soon took their place among the best-educated groups in the United States, with a high number entering white-collar professions. But their new mainstream status and affluence contributed to the weakening of U.S. Catholic identity and practice in the second half of the twentieth century.[44]

For Portier, the dissolution of the subculture was a defining event for twentieth-century American Catholicism, one young people experienced directly. With Catholics now living in the suburbs rather than in traditional urban areas, often with ethnic parishes; fewer going to Catholic schools; more marrying non-Catholics; and Catholic colleges and universities struggling to preserve their religious identity, remaining Catholic becomes increasingly a matter of choice.[45]

A Crisis of Credibility

Andrew Greeley argues that a revolution took place in the United States in the years after the Second Vatican Council. Disillusioned by the inability of the bishops to effectively implement the small reforms made by the council as well as by Pope Paul VI's 1968 encyclical on birth control, Catholics simply stopped listening when Church authorities, expecting blind obedience, attempted to teach on sexuality and other matters requiring acceptance. It was a crisis of credibility. The old wineskins burst, to appropriate Greeley's metaphor.[46]

Greeley also says that Catholics choose to be Catholics on their own terms, though he is more optimistic about young Catholics maintaining a Catholic identity or Catholic imagination.[47] Although most of them reject the sexual ethic of the Church and attend Mass infrequently, the strongest components of their Catholic identity are sacramental, communal, and Marian, and almost half think that the pope is essential.[48]

---

[44] Smith and Denton, *Soul Searching*, 215.

[45] Portier, "Here Come the Evangelical Catholics," 54.

[46] See Greeley, *The Catholic Revolution: New Wine, Old Wineskins, and the Second Vatican Council* (Berkeley: University of California Press, 2004) 192.

[47] Ibid., 110–13.

[48] Ibid., 112–13.

Theological Illiteracy

The theological illiteracy and ignorance of the Catholic tradition that afflicts so many young Catholics may also be a factor in their diminished commitment to the Church. The Notre Dame study of generational differences among Catholics reported that 75 to 80 percent of those in the younger three generations said all major religions are equally good paths to ultimate truth. The study's authors suggest that the tolerance of young Catholics may reflect their attempt to find common ground in a pluralistic world and a Church that encourages openness to other faiths.[49]

Several faculty respondents to the Notre Dame study pointed to an ignorance of Church doctrine as a problem. John Cavadini, chair of Notre Dame's theology department, wondered "how long you can hand down an affection for something when the substance of that very thing becomes fuzzier and fuzzier."[50] In an earlier article he noted that many students, even at elite Catholic colleges and universities, were ignorant of the basic terminology of the faith; accordingly, he called for "a renewed pedagogy of the basics."[51]

Cathleen Kaveny, a professor of law and theology and a post–Vatican II Catholic herself, says that people of her generation didn't learn much doctrine; the catechesis they received "was on engaging our emotions, not on challenging our intellects." With the loss of the coherent Catholic culture of the pre–Vatican II Church, they "do not have the Catholic-in-our-bones sensibilities that characterizes both liberals and conservatives of earlier generations."[52] Mark Poorman, vice president for student affairs at Notre Dame, notes that many of the Catholic students he meets "seem ignorant of the basic theological distinctions, including differences among Christian traditions and between Christianity and other religions; even those who can name the sacraments often cannot articulate a sacramental theology—a central distinguishing tenet of Catholic belief." Interestingly enough, he also observed a strong interest in canon law, perhaps reflecting the need for clarity, concreteness, and boundaries.[53]

---

[49] Davidson and Hoge, "Catholics After the Scandal," 17–18.

[50] John C. Cavadini, "Many Truths? Coming to Terms with Pluralism," *Commonweal* 131/20 (November 19, 2004) 22.

[51] Cavadini, "Ignorant Catholics: The Alarming Void in Religious Education," *Commonweal* 131/7 (April 9, 2004) 13.

[52] Cathleen Kaveny, "Young Catholics: When Labels Don't Fit," *Commonweal* 131/20 (November 19, 2004) 19.

[53] Mark L. Poorman, "A Sign of Hope: Young, Catholic and Curious," *Commonweal* 131/20 (November 19, 2004) 24; see also Steinfels, *A People Adrift,* 204–05.

Michael Gallagher, an Irish Jesuit who has taught literature for twenty years and writes on faith, culture, and spirituality, speaks of "a whole new generation of baptized young adults whose formative experiences with religion or Church are so thin as to be almost non-existent."[54]

This lack of familiarity with their tradition is not a problem just for Catholic university students. The late Monika Hellwig pointed out that those enrolling in ministry programs and even in seminaries often did not have a solid catechetical formation, and even less, an accurate knowledge of common theological terms. "What is often lacking is a common language of the faith, a shared understanding of basic beliefs and practices, and a common memory of the lived experience of the longer tradition." She recommended that there be some kind of remedial introduction to Catholic life, worship, and thought for the students.[55]

My own sense after more than thirty years of teaching Catholic undergraduates is that most of them find it very difficult to give a coherent account of their faith. Most are unfamiliar with the history of the Church, its root metaphors, and its doctrines. Most would not be able to define incarnation, original sin, apostolic succession, or point to any of the principles of Catholic social teaching, though they might mention a "concern for the poor." Unencumbered by a sense of guilt or sin, they do not generally think of Jesus as a savior or redeemer, and they are unfamiliar with the Catholic stories, whether biblical or traditional. Many could not name three sayings of Jesus, do not know the story of St. Paul or any of the saints, particularly contemporary ones, and are usually unfamiliar with Catholic devotions; a considerable number do not know how to pray the rosary. Many are clueless when asked by their Protestant classmates why they bless themselves with holy water, genuflect on entering the church, or pray to Mary. They are as individualistic as their non-Catholic peers, and often relativist in their sense for what is true.

However they do have traditional Catholic sensitivities. Their sense of worship is more liturgical than evangelical, even if they don't go to mass every Sunday. Still, many would be hard pressed to explain what the Church understands by the "real presence" of Christ in the Eucharist. As one student wrote in his essay on the Eucharist, "I had always thought of the Eucharist as a community meal that we all shared symbolizing

---

[54] Michael Paul Gallagher, *Clashing Symbols: An Introduction to Faith and Culture* (New York: Paulist Press, 1998) 112.

[55] Monika Hellwig, "Theology at Catholic Universities: The Situation and its Possibilities," *Origins* 32/43 (2003) 707.

the Last Supper." Although their anthropology is more positive, even optimistic, than the evangelical "total depravity" theology, the students tend toward an implicit rejection of the need for divine intervention for the forgiveness of sin. There is little sense of the reality of sin, or the damage done by what the tradition calls "original sin." As one student said in class, "I can be a good person by myself; why do I need the Church?"

Their imagination is more Catholic than dialectical; while they see God in nature and in other people, few could explain what sacrament or sacramentality means. Their God is kind and benevolent, there when needed, but not someone who enters into their lives with specific calls or demands. What the authors of the UNC study call "Moralistic Therapeutic Deism" certainly fits.[56] These young Catholics have a sense of being part of a universal church and admire the pope as a leader and symbolic representative of Catholicism, but they have little sense of the precise meaning of his office and are almost totally ignorant of his teachings. Their hearts are more Catholic than their intellects.

Conclusion

This profile of young adult Catholics should raise some serious questions about the future vitality of the Catholic community in the United States. First, a diminished institutional commitment to the Catholic Church and to its teaching authority suggests that the Church may continue to lose both influence and members. The decreasing number of those who identify themselves as highly committed to the Church means that a considerable number may leave when faced with a disappointment or personal challenge. Fewer will commit themselves to the priesthood or religious life. And of course, without a strong cohort of strongly committed Catholics, the vitality of the local church will be diminished. At the same time, the fact that most young Catholics seem to have little desire to share their faith with others, in spite of the emphasis on evangelization in the writings of the recent popes, could have a negative impact on the Church's ability to carry out its mission.

The fact that many young Catholics seem to construct their own religious identities on the basis of personal preference also raises the question of the integrity of their Catholic faith and its ability to sustain them.

---

[56] Smith and Denton, *Soul Searching*, 162–63; see above p. 11.

In his concluding homily at World Youth Day at Marienfeld, Cologne (August 2005) the newly elected Pope Benedict XVI cautioned against religion constructed on a "do-it-yourself" basis. Such religion "cannot ultimately help us. It may be comfortable, but at times of crisis we are left to ourselves." The pope pleaded, "Help people to discover the true star which points out the way to us: Jesus Christ!"[57]

Nonetheless, many of the young people who came to take part in World Youth Day and meet the new pope came with an enthusiasm for their faith. Press reports captured something of their vitality and goodness as they endured the cold and damp cheerfully and slept in soggy fields.

Nor are they the only young Catholics whose goodness is evident to others. After years of teaching I continue to be amazed at their respect for each other, their ability to live with considerable diversity in values and lifestyle, and their openness to the new and the unfamiliar. Having grown up with gay friends, they are generally sympathetic to gay people and cannot understand the Vatican's unwillingness to recognize gay unions. As with other Catholics they often have problems with the way authority is exercised in the Church, which we will consider further in the concluding chapter.

The fact that many young Catholics are unfamiliar with the doctrinal tradition of their Church and unable to credibly explain their faith to others remains a problem. They are more ignorant than hostile or disinterested. Even those young Catholics whose affective or emotional attachment to their faith is strong need to become more familiar with the rich cultural and intellectual tradition of the Church. Catholicism is a way of life, not just another church. That way of life begins by cultivating a Catholic imagination.

---

[57] Benedict XVI, "Eucharist: Setting Transformations in Motion," *Origins* 35/12 (2005) 203.

Chapter 2

The Catholic Imagination

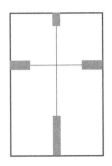

Andrew Greeley has written extensively on what he calls the Catholic imagination, that imaginative faculty that organizes our experience and at the same time becomes a filter that determines *how* we experience our world. He credits David Tracy for supplying the fundamental insight in *The Analogical Imagination,* which contrasts the Catholic sacramental imagination with the Protestant dialectical imagination, focusing in particular on how God is experienced in both traditions.[1] How, then, should we understand the Catholic imagination? What does that imagination have to do with our experience of God and of ourselves as Catholic Christians?

Greeley notes that the imagination is both passive and active. As passive, it is a receptacle or repository of past sensory experiences. As an active power it works creatively or poetically, revealing an active intelligence (the *intellectus agens* of the Aristotelian/Thomistic tradition) that grasps the intelligible by turning to the data of the senses organized by the imagination, in scholastic terms, the phantasm.[2]

The religious imagination has much to do with our experience of the sacred, or God. Its ways of experiencing and describing the divine mystery have been variously characterized: immanence versus transcendence, apophatic versus kataphatic, sacramental (or analogical) versus dialectical. Let me give a couple examples of how our religious imagi-

---

[1] Andrew M. Greeley, *The Catholic Imagination* (Berkeley: University of California Press, 2000) 5; see David Tracy, *The Analogical Imagination: Christian Theology and the Culture of Pluralism* (New York: Crossroad, 1986) 405 ff.

[2] Greeley, *The Religious Imagination* (New York: Sadlier, 1981) 12–16.

nation works, and then try to explore at greater depth the Catholic sacramental imagination.

A good number of years ago I was involved in a Catholic/Lutheran dialogue on Mary in the Church with the distinguished Lutheran New Testament scholar, John Hall Elliott. We talked about Mary in the New Testament, whether her role was primarily historical or symbolic, the different approaches to Mary in our respective Christian traditions, as well as Catholic Marian devotions, doctrine, and apparitions. At the end of the afternoon during the discussion period Professor Elliott asked, "How come Mary never appears to Lutherans?" Right away I answered, "Because Lutherans don't have a Catholic imagination."

The Catholic religious imagination has a strong Marian dimension. Catholics have been praying to Mary as an intercessor since as early as the third century. The ancient intercession known as the *"sub tuum presidium"* invokes her as follows:

> We fly to your protection,
> O holy Mother of God;
> Do not despise us in our need,
> But free us from all evil,
> Most glorious and blessed virgin.

The petition appears in the still-popular *Memorare*, a prayer that dates from the Middle Ages. Mary has long been celebrated in Catholic art and devotion, honored in the Church's liturgy, and recognized in its doctrine. A Catholic church without a statue of Mary is unthinkable.

With the rich Marian devotion that has shaped the Catholic imagination since the earliest days of the Church, it is not surprising that there is a long tradition of apparitions, both official (recognized by the Church) and popular.[3] What are we to make of these apparitions? Karl Rahner argued in his wonderful little book, *Visions and Prophecies*, that a visionary experience or apparition may be a genuine experience of grace, and thus of transcendence, but the imaginative and visual elements come from the imagination of the person claiming the apparition.[4] That imagination will be shaped by the person's religious culture—its traditions,

---

[3] For examples of apparitions in the popular tradition see Mary Lee Nolan and Sidney Nolan, *Christian Pilgrimage in Modern Western Europe* (Chapel Hill, NC: University of North Carolina Press, 1989) 269–89.

[4] Karl Rahner, *Visions and Prophecies* (New York: Herder, 1963) 31–47.

iconography, devotions, and doctrines. What I was trying to say to Professor Elliott was that Lutherans don't have apparitions of Mary because Mary does not generally occupy an important place in their religious imaginations.

Consider another example. Picture a typical Protestant church, let's say a local Baptist or evangelical church, and then compare it with an Italian or Mexican Catholic church. The Protestant church is spare in the extreme—a hall with little ornamentation—dominated by a free-standing pulpit, or perhaps a small table, upon which rests an open Bible. There is little if any art, no icons, no "sacramentals" such as holy water, vigil lights, or statues. Some contemporary Protestant churches are even more functional; think for example of a seeker church hall that looks like a theater or auditorium. It has theater seats, each equipped with holders for the Styrofoam cups of coffee worshipers carry, a stage with amplification equipment for the Jesus rock band, and a proscenium from which the minister will preach.

Now consider a typical Catholic church. Right away there is a different atmosphere. At the doorway, there's a holy water font. Inside, streams of colored light filter through stained glass windows, and vigil lights flicker in front of statues of Mary and the saints—perhaps St. Joseph and St. Thérèse, the Little Flower. A candle burning in a red glass marks the tabernacle, where the reserved presence of Jesus in the Blessed Sacrament is kept. Central to the line of sight is the sanctuary, dominated by the altar, with its candles. Above the altar a large crucifix, perhaps a tortured figure of Jesus showing the wounds of his passion, usually in great detail if the church reflects the Mexican culture. If it is a post–Vatican II church, the art is much more spare and modern, with a separate Blessed Sacrament chapel adjacent to the worship area. But a Catholic church without image or art is difficult to imagine.

John Koessler, a professor of pastoral studies at the Moody Bible Institute in Chicago, in describing his childhood experience of the difference between St. Angela's Catholic Church in his neighborhood and his own Beulah Baptist Church, captures nicely the different emotional impact of the two churches. "St. Angela's seemed to be a dark mystery with its statues of Jesus and Mary and its holy smell. Beulah, on the other hand, met in a plain-looking building, with pale walls and blond furniture. It did not smell holy. No statue of Jesus could be found in the place."[5]

[5] John Koessler, "Why I Return to the Pews," *Christianity Today* 48 (December 2004) 53.

We need to consider the religious imagination more deeply, for our imaginations help put us in touch with the ultimate mystery we call God. First, I'd like to review the affirmative and negative ways of approaching the Ultimate, using some of the great world religions as examples. Second, I would like to consider what has been called the Catholic "sacramental" imagination. Finally, by contrasting Protestant and Catholic expressions of the religious imagination, I would like to suggest how the religious experience out of which a tradition develops takes on imaginative, theological, and ultimately cultural expressions that in turn influence the ways that the members of that tradition experience the divine.

Approaching the Ultimate

Religions that place primary emphasis on the otherness of ultimate reality, its transcendence, tend to follow the apophatic or negative way, the *via negativa* in their theology. They resist representations of God as incomplete or deceptive. Those that experience the divine mystery as immanent are more open to the kataphatic or affirmative way that sees a connection between the material and the spiritual, an analogy between the human and the divine that makes possible a liberal use of the imagination.

For example, Buddhism and Islam generally follow the negative way in their approach to ultimate reality. Buddhism is perhaps the most radical, as it denies that there *is* ultimate reality. Buddhism's goal is to free individuals of "ignorant cravings" and desires. Since both the self and the external world are illusory, the Buddhist seeks Nirvana, the "blowing out" of the flame of passion (Enlightenment), freeing the person from the misery of existence. There is no God, no Creator, no creation, nothing substantial, only the constantly changing present. Wisdom means clinging to nothing, not even Nirvana; it is the realization of emptiness which brings compassion, for every form of egocentricity has been negated.

Islam's doctrine of God stresses the divine transcendence; its monotheism is pure and absolute. Having inherited from Judaism the prohibition of images, Islam teaches that the transcendent God can never be identified with created reality; to do so is to commit the unforgivable sin. Islamic theology uses the language of negation and metaphor, the *via negativa*. In the Qur'an, the eternal, uncreated speech of God comes to earth as text. Islam is generally suspicious of mysticism, though the Sufi tradition is an exception here. For most Muslims, "obeying the will of

God" as it has been revealed in the Qur'an is the way to salvation; thus faithful observance of Islamic law or *Shari'a*, becomes the way of uniting the person to God.

The Jewish religious experience reflected in the Hebrew Scriptures managed to combine both apophatic and kataphatic theologies. Israel's God is both transcendent and near (Jer 23:23). There is clearly a strong apophatic strain evident in the Decalogue's forbidding the fashioning of images "of anything in the sky above or on the earth below or in the waters beneath the earth" (Ex 20:3; cf. Deut 5:8). God dwells in an impenetrable "cloud" (Ex 20:21; 24:15). Israel's monotheism was practical, not speculative; the early books would not have denied the existence of other gods. At the same time, Israel's understanding of God was unique. Nothing in the natural world could represent God; to attempt to do so would detract from the transcendent divine nature, reducing God to something within this world, and thus to the level of the idols of their contemporaries. Israel's prohibition of images of the divine was unique in the Near Eastern culture of its time, and her people struggled against the temptation to assimilate God to one of the forces of nature, particularly the fertility deities worshiped by their neighbors.

But Israel also had a clear sense of the divine immanence. Yahweh was a God present and active in history; God's promise to Israel was always "I will be with you" (Gen 26:3; 31:3; Isa 43:2), and thus God could be encountered through the events of its history, the words and actions of its prophets, and in the retelling of the stories of the people. Because of this sense for God's mediated presence, Israel had a rich tradition of rituals, objects, places, and persons that a Catholic today would recognize as sacramental. While Israel confessed that nothing built by human hands could contain the divine (1 Kgs 8:27), it also saw the Temple as the unique place of God's presence (Ps 68:16-19; Pss 84, 122); it was simply the "house of God" (1 Chr 9:13; Ezra 2:68). And other sacred objects and persons—the sanctuary or Holy of Holies, the Ark of the Covenant, the sacred vessels, rituals of sacrifice and purification, as well as prophets, priests, and kings—all served to mediate God's presence.

Roots of the Catholic Imagination

From its beginning Catholicism combined this sense of God as both transcendent and immanent. Because of the incarnation, Jesus is the very image of the invisible God (Col 1:15), the Word become flesh (John 1:14):

"Whoever has seen me has seen the Father" (John 14:9). Thus, created realities can reflect and image the divine. In Greeley's words, the Catholic imagination "sees the Ultimate lurking in the everyday, in the bits and pieces of everyday life. God discloses himself in water, food and drink, sexual love, birth, death, the touch of a friendly hand, the pale glow of the sun on a frozen winter lake, the sight of a familiar face, long unseen, a Puccini aria, reconciliation after a quarrel, in all the beautiful events and people of human life."[6]

Some argue that a "desacralization" of Christian worship took place among the early Christian communities, as the locus of God's presence shifted from Temple and priesthood to the community itself. Remembering the death and resurrection of Jesus through symbolic expression became more important than the Temple cult. David Power speaks of this as an assimilation of images attached to ritual and its significance into a non-ritualistic context, "thus changing the meaning of the holy."[7]

And yet from very early times Christian communities recognized the disclosure of the holy through ritual actions and artistic images. Rituals, present from the beginning, included the washing of Christian initiation (Acts 2:38-41; 8:36-38), gestures of healing (Acts 3:1-10) that sometimes included an anointing with oil accompanied by prayer (James 5:14), the laying on of hands to communicate the Holy Spirit (Acts 8:17) or to confer a ministry (Acts 6:6; 1 Tim 5:22), and especially the breaking of bread and sharing the cup of wine in memory of Jesus (1 Cor 10:16-17; 11:24-25). The tradition of Christian art has roots that go back to the end of the second or early third century. Among the images found in burial vaults and catacombs are figures from both the Old and New Testaments including Jonah and the great fish, Daniel amidst the lions, and Christ as the Good Shepherd. A chapel in the catacomb of Priscilla has paintings from the end of the second century, a "*fractio panis*" scene representing the Eucharist, another Good Shepherd, an "*Orans*" figure as a symbol of Christian prayer, and what may be an early Madonna and child.[8] Often pagan images were refashioned as Christian symbols.

---

[6] Andrew M. Greeley, *The Catholic Revolution: New Wine, Old Winestains, and the Second Vatican Council* (Berkeley: University of California Press, 2004) 134–35.

[7] David N. Power, *Unsearchable Riches: The Symbolic Nature of Liturgy* (New York: Pueblo, 1984) 37.

[8] John Beckwith, *Early Christian and Byzantine Art* (Baltimore, MD: Penguin Books, 1970; see also André Grabar, *Early Christian Art: From the Rise of Christianity to the Death of Theodosius* (New York: Odyssey Press, 1968).

This disclosure and mediation of the holy through images and ritual was later explicated by Christian theology. To justify the veneration of images, Basil the Great (ca. 330–79) and Athanasius (295–373) distinguished between the image and person represented by the image on the basis of the Platonic relationship between image and archetype,[9] rather like the image from the world of the cave and the idea or form. John Damascene (ca. 675–749), in the midst of controversy over icons, justified their veneration on the basis of the incarnation.[10] The Church Fathers used the Greek *mysterion* and its Latin equivalent, *sacramentum* for a variety of church rites, symbols, ceremonies, blessings, liturgical objects, even feasts. It was only with Peter Lombard (d. 1160) that the number of sacraments was fixed at seven and these were distinguished from "sacramentals": statues, crucifixes, holy water, feasts, and other religious symbols which he described as "signs of grace." One has only to imagine a medieval cathedral, which with its rich statuary, religious art, stained glass, and very architecture stands as a multidimensional symbol of the divine mystery. They have been called "gospels for the illiterate." According to Protestant theologian Langdon Gilkey, this sense of the presence of God though symbols is a continuing Catholic experience "unequalled in other forms of Western Christianity."[11]

At the root of this sense for what we call the sacramental is an emphasis on the incarnation, so strong in eastern Christianity and western Catholicism. Much of Catholic spirituality is kataphatic; God is disclosed in nature, art, and symbol. The visual and the imaginative are prized as aids to contemplation. One thinks immediately of Francis of Assisi's love for nature and for symbols of the story of Jesus such as the Christmas crèche and the cross of San Damiano. Similarly, Ignatius of Loyola emphasized active contemplation of the gospel mysteries in his *Spiritual Exercises*, stressing the composition of place, application of the senses, and repetitions as a way of coming to know and follow Jesus. The final contemplation of the *Exercises*, the "Contemplation to Attain the Love of God," invites individuals to consider the divine gifts of creation, redemption, and favors received, as well as how God dwells in creatures, works and labors in all creatures, and how all these gifts and blessings

---

[9] Hans Belting, *Likeness and Presence: A History of the Image before the Era of Art* (Chicago and London: University of Chicago Press, 1994) 152–53.

[10] John Damascene, *On the Divine Images*, trans. David Anderson (Crestwood, NY: St. Vladimir's Seminary Press, 1980).

[11] Langdon Gilkey, *Catholicism Confronts Modernity* (New York: Seabury Press, 1975) 20.

descend from above, reflecting the divine goodness. The Jesuit impulse of "finding God in all things" is rooted in this vision.

Most of all for Catholicism, with its profoundly incarnational theology, the mystery that veils the invisible nature of God is pierced or disclosed in the humanity of Jesus, the Word become flesh. For Thomas Aquinas,

> by the mystery of the Incarnation are made known at once the goodness, the wisdom, the justice, and the power or might of God—"His goodness, for He did not despise the weakness of His own handiwork; His justice, since, on man's defeat, He caused the tyrant to be overcome by none other than man, and yet He did not snatch men forcibly from death; His wisdom, for He found a suitable discharge for a most heavy debt; His power, or infinite might, for there is nothing greater than for God to become incarnate."[12]

Devotion to the Sacred Heart of Jesus, the often sentimental but profoundly Catholic devotion to the humanity of Jesus, with roots going back to the late Middle Ages, also reflects this tradition.

At the same time, apophatic expressions of spirituality are also present in the Catholic tradition; they can be found in the works of Pseudo-Dionysius in the late fifth or early sixth century, the fourteenth century author of *The Cloud of Unknowing*, as well as in Meister Eckhart (d. 1327), John of the Cross (d. 1591), and Thomas Merton (d. 1968).

Catholic and Protestant Expressions

The theology that emerges out of the foundational religious experience of a tradition continues to shape and define that tradition's religious culture, and thus, the religious experience of its members. But these different emphases find their roots in their different metaphysical foundations. Thomas Aquinas stressed the difference between God as *ipsum esse subsistens*, the sheer act of uncaused existence, and creatures, contingent beings which have being only by participation. Thus created things are beings only in an analogous sense. From this comes the Catholic doctrine of the analogy of being, emphasizing a certain communion between the divine and the created and among created beings themselves, all of which participate in some way in the sheer existence of the

---

[12] Thomas Aquinas, *Summa Theologica*, IIIa, q.1, art. 1; (Benziger Brothers, 1947).

creator. This grounds a belief in the divine immanence as well as the Catholic sacramental imagination.

Protestantism, from its origins in the works of Luther and Calvin, has stressed the transcendence of God. In part this was in reaction to what they saw as abuses in Catholic popular devotion and the Church's sacramental system. And in part this was the inheritance of the late medieval philosophy in which they were trained, with its univocal concept of being and nominalism that were the legacies of Duns Scotus and William of Ockham respectively.[13] Furthermore, Luther's personal struggle over justification or his righteousness before God, has resulted in Protestant theology's stressing the redemption more than the incarnation. This theological orientation has given a profoundly dialogical character to Protestant theology, a concern to emphasize the *difference* between the created, the human, and the divine. Greeley, drawing on Tracy's analysis of dialectical theological language, speaks of the Protestant "dialectical imagination."[14]

Among recent Protestant theologians, few have come closer to a Catholic understanding of theology as a work of the Church than Karl Barth. His *Church Dogmatics* is a massive achievement. Yet Barth's theology differs from Catholic theology precisely because he seeks to carry through to the full the Reformation principles of justification by faith alone and the sovereignty and transcendence of God, or what has been termed the "sovereignty of grace." Because of God's transcendence, Barth vehemently rejects the "*analogia entis*," thus opening a vast chasm between nature and grace, the human and the divine. Indeed, at the beginning of his *Church Dogmatics* he described the Catholic doctrine of the *analogia entis* as the invention of the Antichrist; all other reasons for not becoming Catholic are "shortsighted and lacking in seriousness."[15]

To avoid infringing on God's sovereignty, Barth stresses that grace can never be identified with revelation, the word of Scripture, salvation, or the Church, whether in its preaching, sacramental signs, or structures; grace cannot be domesticated. His insistence on the contingent and epi-

---

[13] See Colin E. Gunton, *The One, the Three and the Many: God, Creation, and the Culture of Modernity* (Cambridge: Cambridge University Press, 1993) 56–58; also Robert Barron's fine essay, "The Christian Humanism of Karol Wojtyla and Thomas Aquinas," in his *Bridging the Great Divide: Musings of a Post-Liberal, Post-Conservative Evangelical Catholic* (Lanham, MD: Rowman & Littlefield Publishers, 2004).

[14] Greeley, *The Catholic Imagination*, 8; cf. David Tracy, *The Analogical Imagination*, 405 ff.

[15] Karl Barth, *Church Dogmatics*, ed. by G. W. Bromiley and T. F. Torrance (Edinburgh: T. & T. Clark), I/I *The Doctrine of God* (1936) x; henceforth *CD*.

sodic character of these realities is designed to protect God's sovereign freedom, but Barth tends to dissolve them into a series of discrete happenings, actualized in moments through the Spirit's action. In Robert Cushman's words, "so jealous is he for the Lordship of God that he will not allow the Holy Ghost to 'come to roost' in human life in such a way as that his action and presence is manifest in the texture and shape of historical personality."[16] Contrast this with the Catholic emphasis on God's faithfulness to the community of believers through the sacraments (*ex opere operato*) and on its magisterial teaching authority (infallibility).

Barth's theology, with its emphasis on act over being, has been described as "actualism."[17] The chasm he sees between nature and grace rules out any elevation of created reality, no transformation on the basis of the incarnation. Nature is fallen and corrupt. Created realities cannot image the divine. Human beings are not "open" to God and cannot cooperate with God's grace. The Church is not constantly the Church, but only in its momentary transformation by the Spirit. Barth goes so far as to say that Catholic devotion to the Sacred Heart of Jesus represents an illegitimate "deification of the creature"[18] and he argues that "where Mary is 'venerated,' . . . there the Church of Christ is not."[19]

I have focused at some length on Barth because of his concern to give the foundational Reformation principles their full due in his theology and because they show the continuing effect of these principles on the classical Protestant imagination. In a similar way, Robert Barron argues that the Protestant fudging of the distinction as well as the rapport between God and the universe and its misunderstanding of the God-world relationship expressed in the *analogia entis* paved the way for what he calls its "secular counterpart, philosophical modernity."[20] Let me try now to parse out the effects of these different Catholic and Protestant imaginations, based on their different fundamental theological visions.

With its emphasis on the incarnation and thus, on the divine presence in creation, Catholic theology in the sixteenth century was able to maintain a more optimistic anthropology despite its own Augustinian inheritance and the soteriological concerns of day. Human nature is damaged by original sin, but the image of God remains. Human beings can know

[16] Robert E. Cushman, "Karl Barth on the Holy Spirit," *Religion in Life* 24 (1955) 574.

[17] Avery Dulles, "The Church, the Churches, and the Catholic Church," *Theological Studies* 33 (1972) 205–06; also Colm O'Grady, *The Church in Catholic Theology: Dialogue with Karl Barth* (London: Geoffrey Chapman, 1969).

[18] Barth, CD I/2 (1956) 138.

[19] Ibid., 143.

[20] See Barron, *Bridging the Great Divide*, 107–14, at 112.

that God exists from creation and must cooperate with God's grace. Human freedom is taken seriously. God can be encountered in nature, persons, community, and sacramental signs as well as in Scripture. Because of its primary emphasis on the incarnation, Catholic theology is more mystical; an immanent God can be experienced. Humanity in all its concreteness is the bearer of the divine. Catholicism's appreciation for art and metaphor as well as a rich devotional life is reflected in its sacramental or analogical imagination.

Protestant theological anthropology is much more pessimistic. Its primary doctrinal emphasis is on the redemption. This fundamental soteriological concern highlights the effects of original sin, resulting in a view of human nature as "totally corrupt," as Calvin said. The intellect is blinded, unable to know God apart from grace, and the will is in bondage, incapable of choosing the good. For Calvin, even infants are guilty, "not of another's fault but of their own . . . their whole nature is a seed of sin; hence it can be only hateful and abhorrent to God."[21] The logical result of this was Calvin's doctrine of double predestination—the divine determination that some will be saved and some will be damned. These different theological starting points, and the different anthropologies they lead to, affect the way God is known and experienced in both traditions. Let's consider these different theologies on three points: whether God is distant (transcendent) or near (immanent) to us; how God is known, and what role art might play in our religious experience.

1. *Is God transcendent or immanent?* With its great emphasis on the incarnation, Catholic thought and spirituality emphasizes the divine immanence. God is immanent to his creation, reflected in its beauty, and known from his works. Creation is good, marriage is a sacrament revealing God's love, and social structures and governments are good, serving the common good. Even the saints are still close to us; because they and we share in the divine life, we can invoke their intercession, something Protestants do not understand and reject as unbiblical. Catholicism speaks of this as the communion of saints.

From the Protestant perspective, the emphasis is on the divine transcendence, especially where Calvin's theology still rules. Unlike the Catholic tradition, which sees grace building on nature, for traditional Protestantism, there is a chasm between nature and grace; this rules out any elevation of created reality on the basis of the incarnation. Nature

---

[21] John Calvin, *Institutes*, II,1,8; see *Institutes of the Christian Religion*, Library of Christian Classics, Vol. XX, ed. John T. McNeill (Philadelphia: Westminster, 1960) 251.

is fallen and corrupt. Created realities cannot image the divine. Christ's sacrifice means that our sins have been "covered over," not taken away, and Christ's righteousness attributed to us (forensic justification). Human beings are not "open" to God and cannot cooperate with God's grace. The Church is not constantly the Church, but only in its momentary transformation by the Spirit, while the real Church is invisible.

These contrasting theologies have important consequences for social theory. Barron sees modernity as a secularized form of Protestantism in which the transcendent God of Luther ultimately disappeared entirely. "Where Aquinas, in line with his participation metaphysics, held society as natural to human beings, Hobbes saw humans in a natural state as simply antagonistic individuals, set violently against one another." It was this Hobbsian view, tempered by John Locke, that shaped the liberal democracies of the eighteenth century. Given a hostile view of society as a group of self-interested individuals, government's purpose becomes the defense of individual rights, not the protection of the common good of society needed for human flourishing.[22] Catholic ethical concerns tend toward communalism, Protestant toward individualism.[23]

Of course Protestants also recognize that God is present and active in the world; evangelicals in particular stress a supernaturalism open to divine interventions, miraculous healings, and personal revelations. Thus they, too, believe that God is immanent, and Catholics also believe that God is transcendent. What I'm referring to here is the perspective most emphasized in both traditions, which in turn impacts how God is experienced.

2. *How is God known?* The Protestant doctrine of the total corruption of human nature affects the way humans come to know God. For Protestant theology, because of the corruption of human nature and its faculties, there is no "natural" knowledge of God. God can be known only through Scripture, "*sola Scriptura*," through the intervention of the prophetic word. Whereas Catholicism has a rich tradition of mystical prayer, Protestantism is generally more prophetic than mystical.

3. *The place of metaphor and art.* Although Luther rejected a body/spirit dualism and saw the value of material signs in worship,[24] Reformation

---

[22] Barron, *Bridging the Great Divide*, 134.

[23] Greeley, *The Catholic Imagination*, 130–31.

[24] Carlos M. N. Eire, *War against the Idols: The Reformation of Worship from Erasmus to Calvin* (Cambridge: Cambridge University Press, 1986) 70–73.

theology in general tends to be wary of the abuse of metaphor and sees in religious images a temptation to idolatry.

In the classical Reformation this suspicion of religious images led to widespread destruction of sacred images, to a "stripping of the altars,"[25] particularly in those countries where Calvin's theology flourished. Iconoclasm was a force in Switzerland even before Calvin came to Geneva in 1536, and it was more than a protest against the rituals and imagery of Catholicism. Iconoclasm was rooted in Protestant theology, in what Carlos Eire calls its "transcendentalist spirit" and "otherworldly emphasis."[26] But Calvin's emphasis on the divine transcendence, on the incapacity of the finite for the infinite (*finitum non est capax infiniti*), was to indelibly stamp Reformed theology and worship,[27] and thus, the way Christians in the Reformed tradition experience the divine. Call to mind our meditation on the two different church buildings.

Andrew Greeley's *The Catholic Imagination* explores the varied ways that Catholicism's appreciation for the symbolic and metaphorical influences the way Catholics come to know and experience God. Art, human sexual love, churches as sacred places ("if there are no votive candles in it, a church really isn't Catholic"),[28] the celebration of the sexuality of Jesus in Renaissance painting, graphically evident in Leo Steinberg's fascinating book as an expression of the capacity of the human to bear the divine,[29] Mariology as a symbol of the tenderness of God, literature, and film—all this is what Greeley calls "the popular tradition" of Catholicism, more richly developed than in Judaism, Protestantism, and Islam, the other three religions of the book, because Catholicism "is least afraid of the imaginative dimension of religion."[30]

Unfortunately, some have seen a similar "stripping of the altars" in post–Vatican II liberal Catholicism. Robert Barron sees in the present tendency to strip contemporary Catholic churches of devotional art, statues, crucifixes, and vigil lights, draining them of color and the play of light and darkness, redefining them as worship spaces as an expression of the Cartesian spirit of modernity: "the emptied-out, assembly-centric ecclesial building is symbolically inadequate. In the great tradition

---

[25] Eamon Duffy, *The Stripping of the Altars: Traditional Religion in England c. 1400–c. 1580* (New Haven and London: Yale University Press, 1992).

[26] Eire, *War Against the Idols*, 142–43.

[27] Ibid., 197–202.

[28] Greeley, *The Catholic Imagination*, 34.

[29] See Leo Steinberg, *The Sexuality of Christ in Renaissance Art and in Modern Oblivion* (New York: Pantheon, 1982).

[30] Greeley, *The Catholic Imagination*, 77.

of Catholic ecclesial architecture, church structures are decidedly not simply gathering spaces, but rather repositories of the Christian story and therefore conduits to an entirely new world of psychological and religious experience."[31]

At its best, because of its appreciation for the metaphorical and the symbolic, Catholicism is more ready to recognize the capacity of popular art and culture to disclose the divine. For example, David Brading's recent study of Our Lady of Guadalupe argues: "as much as any icon, the Virgin of Tepeyac silently taught the truths of revelation as effectively as scripture since, like the gospels, the image was conceived through the inspiration of the Holy Spirit."[32] Whether the image was produced miraculously or by human creativity is immaterial to Brading, for he recognizes that both the Scriptures and religious icons are the works of humans open to and moved by the Spirit.

I experienced this Catholic appreciation for the revelatory capacity of popular art a few years ago. I was a participant in a forum on "Evangelicals, Catholics, and the Entertainment Media," sponsored by the City of the Angles Film Festival in Los Angeles (November 12, 2001). In the discussion it became apparent that the Catholic approach to film was quite different from that of evangelical Protestants. Catholics, with their sense for sacramentality, easily see cinematic images and stories as disclosing the presence of grace, whether named or not. Greeley's book offers many examples of this in his analysis of films such as Lars von Trier's *Breaking the Waves* and Martin Scorsese's *Mean Streets*. He writes that "Catholic artists and writers tend to hunger for the salvation of their characters . . . because they find themselves in a grace-filled world."[33] I experienced this powerfully in a class, as I was trying to explain how grace is mediated by persons and symbols. The students just didn't get it until one of them mentioned the fine film "Dead Man Walking" about a man on Death Row. The condemned man, played by Sean Penn, at the last moment seems to open himself to the grace brought to him in the love and ministry of Sister Helen Prejean, even though he does not call on the name of Jesus and confess his sins. As the student talked about the film, the others in the class began nodding their heads. They'd all seen the film and they got it.

[31] Barron, *Bridging the Great Divide*, 76; see also Greeley, *The Catholic Revolution*, 81–89.

[32] David A. Brading, *Mexican Phoenix: Our Lady of Guadalupe: Image and Tradition Across Five Centuries* (Cambridge: Cambridge University Press, 2001) 366.

[33] Greeley, *The Catholic Imagination*, 168.

Evangelicals, with their emphasis on the proclamation of the word, generally have a more literal approach to cinema. A film is a vehicle to evangelize individuals, to carry out the Great Commission to convey the Christian message to the world. Thus if an evangelical were making a film about an encounter with grace, it would most likely be an explicitly religious story. As panelist Robert Johnston, an evangelical professor at Fuller Theological Seminary observed, though evangelicals "can talk about God being alive and active in the world, we have tended to underplay the value of common grace."[34]

If we were to try to represent the differences between the two expressions of the religious imagination that we've been considering graphically, it might look something like this:

Catholic Imagination	Protestant Imagination
Emphasis on **incarnation:** stress on God's **immanence** to created reality; creation is good	Emphasis on **redemption:** stress on God's **transcendence**
Anthropology: human nature is created in God's image, damaged by original sin but image of God remains; human beings can know that God exists from creation and must cooperate with God's grace	**Anthropology:** human nature "totally corrupt" because of original sin, intellect blinded, will in bondage; no knowledge of God, apart from grace, human beings incapable of good; predestination
God encountered: in nature, Scripture, persons, community; sacramental signs	**God encountered:** through proclamation of God's Word; stresses biblical word, judgment
Mystical: God can be experienced	**Prophetic:** God is revealed in Scripture
Stresses God's presence in world	Stresses God's distance from world
Liberal use of metaphor (God is like)	Wary of metaphor (God is other)
Love of religious art, artifacts, devotions	Classical Reformation rejected religious art as temptation to idolatry
Communitarian: stresses the common good; society is natural and good, needed for human flourishing; emphasis on community; natural law	**Individualistic:** stresses individual rights; society is unnatural and oppressive; individual realizes full humanity by becoming completely free; social contract

---

[34] For an evangelical appreciation of popular culture see William D. Romanowski, *Eyes Open: Looking for God in Popular Culture* (Grand Rapids, MI: Brazos Press, 2001).

Conclusion

In this chapter I have tried to show how Catholics and Protestants have remarkably different religious imaginations because of the circumstances of their origins and the influence of their formative figures. The Catholic sacramental imagination is rooted in early Christianity's Jewish heritage which, in spite of its strong sense for the divine transcendence, was able to recognize God's presence in its history, its sacred figures, and its cult. Protestant Christianity from its origins chose to emphasize the divine transcendence, in no small measure as a reaction to or "protest" against Catholic sacramentalism and its whole system of mediation.

This does not mean that Protestants never come to a sense of God's closeness, mediated by their ordinary experience, or that the imagination plays little role in their religious life. Robert Wuthnow, in a chapter titled "Redeeming the Religious Imagination," writes: "The historic disjuncture between religion and the imagination—what historian Karen Armstrong has termed an 'excessively theoretical and limiting cast of mind in Western theology'—appears to be breaking down."[35] But if a religious tradition does not suggest the possibility of encountering the divine in nature, art, story, and ritual, those shaped by its culture will be far less likely to experience them as mediating the divine presence, for our religious cultures function as hermeneutical or interpretative frameworks.

Our imaginations, and thus, the way we experience the divine, are shaped by those cultures and the theologies they both express and give rise to. Just as Protestants don't experience apparitions of Mary, most Catholics don't talk about having the "born again" experience so prized by evangelicals. This is not because they have no real experience of a personal relationship with Jesus, but because their Catholic religious culture neither prepares them for this "evangelical" experience, nor supplies the imaginative language to describe it. They have a different religious imagination.

---

[35] See Robert Wuthnow, *All in Sync: How Music and Art Are Revitalizing American Religion* (Berkeley: University of California Press, 2003) 184; Armstrong is quoted in "Report on the 3rd International Conference on Religion, Literature, and the Arts," *Religion, Literature, and the Arts Newsletter* 1 (March 7, 1996) 1.

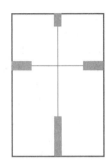

Chapter 3

The Catholic Tradition and
The Da Vinci Code

Some time ago I was asked by our local pastor to prepare a talk on Dan Brown's bestselling novel, *The Da Vinci Code*. Initially I resisted. In spite of the book's enormous popularity—some forty million copies sold worldwide—I found the writing so far-fetched and unbelievable in its development that I didn't want to invest the time. I felt it would be like trying to critique a fairy tale. As many point out, it's just a novel, pure fiction, a page turner that most readers can't put down. The trouble is that many people, unfamiliar with the origins of the Church, the shaping of the Christian tradition, or simply history, tend to accept uncritically much of what Brown says. For example, his statement that the Church in a 300 year period burned at the stake some five million women for witchcraft.

But I finally did the talk, and I'm glad that I did. It's always educational to review the story of the Church's origins, and the book is more than a work of fiction. In presenting the Catholic Church as the enemy of truth Brown is attacking not just the Church, but also the canon of Scripture and the doctrines of salvation, Christology, and the Trinity that are the Church's legacy. In other words, Christianity itself.

There is much to tantalize the reader in Brown's book. The main characters are a scholarly Harvard professor, Robert Langdon, and Sophie Neveu, an attractive French cryptologist, whose not very subtle name means the "new wisdom," and who, as it turns out, is descended from Jesus. They discover a secret capable of destroying the Catholic Church (the only church Brown seems interested in) and engage in an ongoing intrigue between Opus Dei and a newly liberal Vatican. There's also a murderous Opus Dei "numerary" who purifies himself with a sharp circle of barbs worn on his thigh and a little whip or discipline.

Conspiracy theorists love it. It has just enough scholarly controversies to give it verisimilitude. The Church has indeed often been fearful of sex and spoken disparagingly of women, and there are some Gnostic texts that describe Gnostic communities in which women and men functioned as equals in the liturgy. Some feminist theologians have spoken of the book appreciatively because of its celebration of the "sacred feminine," in contrast to what seems to be the fear of women in the Church. What is most amazing, however, is that so many have taken the book seriously.

First of all, *The Da Vinci Code* is no way original; nor is it based on facts, as Brown claims. It is based on a number of earlier, questionable works, none of them scholarly. Secondly, with its enthusiasm for Gnosticism and the Gnostic literature, the book strikes an appealing chord for many people today in advocating, not historic Christianity with its doctrinal tradition and incarnational faith, but a subjective spirituality more appropriate for a spiritual elite. Arguing that the Gnostic gospels are earlier than the canonical gospels, Brown reduces the divinity of Jesus, and thus the doctrine of the incarnation, to a political plot by the Roman Emperor Constantine, forced on the Council of Nicaea (325) to unify his empire by making salvation available only through a single sacred channel, the now established Catholic Church with its hierarchical structure.[1] Third, at the heart of Brown's book is his story of a sexual relationship between Jesus and Mary Magdalene resulting in descendents surviving down to modern times, a story suppressed by the Church because it would threaten its doctrine of the divinity of Jesus.

Questionable Sources

The Da Vinci Code's appearance has generated a cottage industry of refutations, with more than a dozen books listed on Amazon.com. Interestingly enough, Brown's book has brought Catholic and evangelical Christians together in refuting what is recognized by all as an attack on the substance of the Christian faith. Darrell Bock, in his helpful book, refers to the early "tradition-based Christians," an interesting expression for an evangelical scholar, as evangelicals usually follow a "Scripture alone" approach.[2] The work of another evangelical biblical scholar, Ben

---

[1] Dan Brown, *The Da Vinci Code* (New York: Doubleday, 2003) 233.

[2] Darrell L. Bock, *Breaking the Da Vinci Code* (Nashville, TN: Thomas Nelson, 2004) 97.

Witherington III's *The Gospel Code*, is particularly good for addressing many of the biblical arguments in Brown's work.[3] Also, the work by Carl E. Olson and Sandra Miesel, *The Da Vinci Hoax*, offers considerable background on the bogus sources of Brown's book, as well as a careful analysis of his artistic interpretations.[4]

Brown relies on a number of highly imaginative, non-scholarly sources, particularly a book published in 1982 called *Holy Blood, Holy Grail* that outlines the essential story Brown tells—the discovery that Jesus with Mary Magdalene, the real "Holy Grail," fathered children whose blood line continues down through the centuries. The story was supposedly discovered by the Knights Templar who unearthed secret documents from beneath the ruins of the Temple of Jerusalem, becoming enormously powerful until they were destroyed by a jealous pope. Their secret was allegedly preserved by the Priory of Sion which ultimately attempted to set the offspring of this "royal" bloodline on the throne of France.[5]

The three authors, two of whose names Brown reproduces as anagrams for his own characters, are neither historians nor theologians; one is a BBC television producer, another an American novelist with a degree in comparative literature, the third an Australian photographer and psychologist. One scholar, in a review entitled "Raiders of the Lost Grail," points out that the authors "admit repeatedly that they have no real evidence, only a hypothesis."[6] They were dependent on the fictitious story of the Priory of Sion, created by Pierre Plantard, a French anti-Semite and reactionary who served six months in jail for fraud and embezzlement in 1953 and ultimately claimed to be himself the true king of France.

Brown also relies heavily on a book called *The Templar Revelation*, but this work dismisses the *Dossier Secrets*, supposedly the secret papers of the Priory of Sion, as fabrications.[7] Another predecessor is Margaret

---

[3] Ben Witherington, III, *The Gospel Code; Novel Claims About Jesus, Mary Madgalene and Da Vinci* (Downers Grove, IL: InterVarsity, 2004).

[4] Carl E. Olson and Sandra Miesel, *The Da Vinci Hoax: Exposing the Errors in the Da Vinci Code* (San Francisco: Ignatius Press, 2004).

[5] Michael Baigent, Richard Leigh, and Henry Lincoln, *Holy Blood, Holy Grail* (New York: Dell, 1983).

[6] Tom Sinclair Faulkner "Raiders of the Lost Grail" *The Christian Century* 99/27 (September 1 and 8, 1982) 892.

[7] Lynn Picknett and Clive Prince, *The Templar Revelation: Secret Guardians of the True Identity of Christ* (New York: Simon and Schuster, 1998) 39–57; see Olson and Miesel, *The Da Vinci Hoax*, 228.

Starbird's *The Woman with the Alabaster Jar: Mary Magadalen and the Holy Grail*.[8] A former Catholic religious educator who confuses Mary Magdalene with Mary of Bethany, she admits to being won over to the "theories" set forth in *Holy Blood, Holy Grail*.[9] Starbird has since written two other books on the recovery of the sacred feminine, the latest decoding the symbolic numbers she finds embedded in the original Greek phrases of the New Testament. None of these works count as credible historical studies. In sum, *The Da Vinci Code* is based on a number of fictitious, self-contradicting sources.

The Church's Struggle with Gnosticism

Much more interesting than these sources is the story of the early Church's struggle with Gnosticism and its heterodox literature which drew freely on Christian sources. The struggle with Gnosticism was one of the greatest challenges faced by the early Church. Brown, like some other contemporary authors, wants to include the Gnostic works as representative of other, equally legitimate forms of early Christianity.[10] Let's look specifically at a number of charges Brown makes in *The Da Vinci Code:* his contentions that Constantine forced the Council of Nicaea to declare Jesus divine, his claim that the Gnostic literature is earlier than the canonical gospels, and his assertion that Gnosticism exalts the sacred feminine.

Constantine and Jesus' Divinity

Brown inflates enormously the role of the Roman Emperor Constantine. He implies that Constantine was responsible for the Council of Nicaea's proclaiming Jesus as the divine Son of God, a tactical move to unify his fractious empire (231–234). His character, Leigh Teabing says that until Nicaea "Jesus was viewed by His followers as a moral prophet . . . a

---

[8] Margaret Starbird, *The Woman with the Alabaster Jar: Mary Magadalen and the Holy Grail* (Rochester, VT: Bear, 1993).

[9] See Olson and Miesel, 53, note 19.

[10] See Elaine Pagels, *The Gnostic Gospels* (New York: Random House, 1989); also Bart D. Ehrman, *Lost Christianities: The Battles for Scripture and the Faiths We Never Knew* (Oxford/New York: Oxford University Press, 2003); also *Lost Scriptures: Books That Did Not Make it into the New Testament*, ed. Ehrman (Oxford/New York: Oxford University Press, 2003).

great and powerful man, but a *man* nonetheless" (233). This shows either enormous ignorance of or simple disregard for the New Testament. It is true that there are a rich variety of Christologies in the New Testament, not all of them asserting the divinity of Jesus. It is also true that as the early Christians struggled to express their experience of Jesus in light of their monotheistic Jewish faith, there are numerous expressions of their belief that Jesus is more than a man, all of this in the first century.

There is considerable evidence that the very early communities made Jesus an object of devotion, singing hymns and addressing prayers to him, invoking him during their worship or liturgy, baptizing in his name, and of course, celebrating the Eucharist; in other words, making him the object of the devotion traditionally reserved to God.[11] From the beginning the early Christians addressed Jesus as "Lord," the Greek *kyrios* used in the Septuagint Greek translation of the Old Testament to translate the holy name of Yahweh. The significance of this that would not have been lost on early Jewish Christians. The Wisdom tradition, with its feminine personification of Wisdom (Prov 1, 8, 9; Sirach 24; Wis 7–9; Baruch 3:9–4:4), coming forth from God (Sirach 24:3; Prov 8:22-23), playing a role in creation (Prov 8:25-31; Sirach 1:4; Wis 7:22; 9:9), and having a mission to God's people (Wis 6:12-16; 9:10-18; 10-12) seems to have played an important role in attributing preexistence to Jesus, perhaps as early as Paul.

A Christology suggesting the preexistence of Jesus is suggested in Paul's letter to the Philippians (ca. 54), where he says "though he was in the form of God, he did not regard equality with God something to be grasped. Rather he emptied himself, taking the form of a slave, coming in human likeness, and found human in appearance" (Phil 2:6-7; cf. 2 Cor 8–9). Some scholars consider the meaning of this text as still subject to dispute, but an increasing number of scholars see the text as affirming Christ's preexistence.[12]

The Gospel of John has a high Christology. In the Prologue, Jesus is proclaimed the eternal Word become flesh. The gospel's author repeatedly uses the divine formula "I am," the Greek *ego eimi*. In the Septuagint, this is used to translate the Hebrew revelatory formula "I am Yahweh" (Exod 6:7). The gospel culminates with Thomas' great confession of faith before the risen Jesus as "My Lord and my God" (John 20:28), one of the few times in the New Testament that the word "God" is predicated of

---

[11] See Larry W. Hurtado, *One God, One Lord: Early Christian Devotion and Ancient Jewish Monotheism* (Philadelphia: Fortress, 1988) 99–114.

[12] Cf. Roger Haight, *Jesus Symbol of God* (Maryknoll, NY: Orbis, 1999) 169.

Jesus. Belief in Jesus' divinity is evident in the writing of the fathers of the Church prior to Nicaea. When the bishops assembled at Nicaea, a council summoned by the Emperor Constantine, it was not to create a new doctrine, but to safeguard the faith of the Church against the heresy of Arius (b. 256), who taught that Jesus was "the first born of all creation" but still a creature. In Gerald O'Collins' words, Nicaea "did not invent faith in Christ's divinity but added another (semi-philosophical) way of confessing it."[13]

Behind the controversies which led to Nicaea's confession and would continue until Chalcedon in 451 was the problem of trying to find the theological language that would do full justice to the Church's faith that Jesus, while fully human, was also divine, making clear the presence of God in Jesus and in the world. Some theologians have argued that Nicaea and Chalcedon represented an illegitimate Hellenizing of Christianity, divinizing the man Jesus. But a much better case can be made that the christological controversies of the fourth and fifth centuries transformed the Greek philosophical way of thinking, which has so influenced our own. Rather than seeing impersonal universal nature as the supreme reality—Plato's forms or Aristotle's universals—through the influence of Christianity the most real would be seen as the existing individual substance, and ultimately, as personal.[14]

The Priority of the Gnostic Gospels

Were the Gnostic gospels written earlier than the canonical gospels? The canonical gospels were all written before the end of the first century, and most of the rest of the New Testament for that matter. A few Gnostic works like the Gospel of Thomas may have come from the early second century, though a date after 150 is more likely for most of them. The claim made by Brown's character Teabing in the book that "eighty gospels were considered for the New Testament, and yet only a relatively few were chosen for inclusion—Matthew, Mark, Luke, and John among them" (231) is simply ridiculous. And the idea that Constantine commissioned a new Bible, destroying the earlier Gnostic gospels (234) is difficult to maintain. Yet the idea that Constantine was responsible for the canon has grown in recent years, and so Dan Brown is not alone in alleging

---

[13] "The Da Vinci Code," *America* 189/20 (Dec. 15, 2003) 16.

[14] Thomas P. Rausch, *Who Is Jesus? An Introduction to Christology* (Collegeville, MN: Liturgical Press, 2003) 163–64.

this. Much of this is due to the controversial Jesus Seminar, which has produced a collection of twenty texts called *The Complete Gospels*,[15] as well as John Dominic Crossan, who argued on the A&E television documentary, *Christianity: the First Thousand Years*, that Constantine's commissioning of fifty great Bibles for the empire played a major role.[16] And it is true that once Christianity became established in the Roman Empire (313–81), most copies of the Gnostic scriptures were banned and destroyed as they had long been considered heretical.[17]

The process of establishing the New Testament canon is a fascinating one. It was precisely the growing problem of false teachers (look at the frequent warnings against false teachers in 1 and 2 Timothy and Titus, documents written toward the end of the New Testament period) and later, the appearance of nonorthodox, often Gnostic religious writings using Christian symbolism and concepts that led to the gradual development of the canon. The criteria for accepting a work into what became the canon were apostolic authority (hence the number of NT works attributed to an apostle), wide usage in the churches, and the ability of a work to reflect the Church's faith. Catholics love to point this out to evangelicals; it was the Catholic Church that gave us the New Testament Scriptures. As the community's faith was challenged and spurious texts appeared, the Church was forced to define and make clearer the parameters of its faith.

It's true that some members of the Jesus Seminar assign early dates to some Gnostic works, but few scholars take their work seriously. For example, Crossan depends heavily on "first editions" of the Gospel of Thomas, the Gospel of Peter, the Cross Gospel, and the Secret Gospel of Mark. In his study, *Hidden Gospels: How the Search for Jesus Lost Its Way*, Philip Jenkins argues that the dates for the noncanonical texts used by the Jesus Seminar are "improbably early."[18] None of the early writings mention the Cross Gospel or any early version of Peter.[19] Although the Gospel of Thomas includes some sayings that may go back to Jesus, according to Bart Ehrman the document itself reflects Gnostic teachings that cannot be dated prior to the beginning of the second century; "the

[15] Ed. Robert J. Miller (Sonoma: Polebridge Press, 1992).

[16] See Philip Jenkins, *Hidden Gospels: How the Search for Jesus Lost Its Way* (New York: Oxford University Press, 2001) 84–87.

[17] Bentley Layton, *The Gnostic Scriptures* (New York: Doubleday, 1987) xi.

[18] See Jenkins, *Hidden Gospels*, 95.

[19] Ibid., 96.

document as a whole probably came to be written sometime after the New Testament Gospels . . ., possibly in the early second century."[20] John P. Meier, in his massive work, *A Marginal Jew*, says that the Gospel of Peter is "a [second] century pastiche of traditions from the canonical Gospels . . . and has no special access to early independent tradition about the historical Jesus."[21] He argues that Crossan's failure to make a case for the Gospel of Peter makes very dubious his claims for the priority of the other apocryphal gospels he relies on.

Thus the evidence indicates that the Gnostic gospels, rather than being earlier than the canonical gospels, are clearly later and often dependent on the canonical gospels. The heretic Marcion (ca. 150), Justin Martyr in Rome (ca. 150), and Tatian (ca. 170) all refer to the traditional four gospels, indicating an accepted tradition. About 170, the Syrian Tatian harmonized the traditional four gospels in his *Diatessaron*. While his work was problematic, rather like Mel Gibson's attempt to combine four different gospel stories into one in his film, *The Passion of the Christ*, it does indicate that by 170, long before Constantine, there was an already accepted tradition of four gospels, Matthew, Mark, Luke, and John.

The Doctrine of Salvation

One of the most significant differences between the Gnostic literature and that of the orthodox Christian communities was that for Gnosticism, like some modern Gnostic movements, salvation was understood as personal enlightenment for a spiritual elite, a "secret knowledge" (*gnosis* in Greek) mediated by the Gnostic literature. In some ways, historic Gnosticism is surprisingly contemporary. The Gnostics saw the major spiritual problem as not sin, but ignorance.[22] Orthodox Christianity, on the other hand, proclaimed the saving story of the life, death, and resurrection of Jesus as a liberating and transforming message. It was not a secret knowledge for a spiritual elite, but essentially public and missionary, good news for all to hear. As Elaine Pagels, who prefers Gnostic to orthodox Christianity, notes, "[o]rthodox Christians were concerned—far more than gnostics—with their relationships with other people."[23]

---

[20] Ehrman, *Lost Scriptures*, 20.

[21] John P. Meier, *A Marginal Jew: Rethinking the Historical Jesus*, I. *The Roots of the Problem and the Person* (New York: Doubleday, 1991) 117–18.

[22] Bock, *Breaking the Da Vinci Code*, 83.

[23] Pagels, *The Gnostic Gospels*, 146.

An important admission; Christianity was other-oriented! If Gnosticism was a solitary faith for an elite, orthodox Christianity was and is essentially communal. Perhaps this is why Gnosticism and its contemporary expressions are so popular today in our individualistic, postmodern culture, particularly with those who like to say "I'm spiritual, but not religious."

Gnosticism and the Sacred Feminine

One of Dan Brown's most seductive arguments is that the Gnostic gospels promote an exalted view of women, a view of the "sacred feminine," later suppressed by the Church. A number of recent, neo-Gnostic feminist works have sought to make this argument.[24] However, a careful reading of the Gnostic literature makes it extremely dubious.

The issue is complicated, for there were diverse Gnostic traditions. The earliest Gnostics, writing in the mid-second century, interpreted the Old and New Testaments in a way that was hostile to the God of Israel, to the resurrection, the reality of Jesus' incarnation and suffering, and the universality of Christian salvation. For this heavily Greek mentality, the idea of God taking on flesh and suffering was repugnant, but it lies at the heart of orthodox Christianity. Valentinus was more open to what Layton calls "proto-orthodox Christianity, but still essential Gnostic himself.[25] In communities influenced by Valentinian Gnosticism and probably others, women appear to have had equal standing in the cult, taking on leading roles denied them in the official Church.[26] And some Gnostic texts speak of a God who embraces both masculine and feminine elements.[27] Though as Bock suggests, this is to portray God in humanity's image, rather than humanity in the image of God.[28]

Other Gnostic traditions taught that Satan, not God, made the world. These traditions denigrated women, rejecting marriage and sexual relationships as defiling. The very division of the sexes into male and female was seen as the mark of a lost unity, the fault of Eve, thus of woman. Surveying the literature, Kurt Rudolf concludes, "in the final analysis

---

[24] Olson and Miesel, *The Da Vinci Hoax*, mention Eileen Pagels, Margaret Starbird, Merlin Stone, and Riane Eisler, 90.

[25] See Layton, *The Gnostic Scriptures*, xxii.

[26] See Kurt Rudolph, *Gnosis*, trans. and ed. by Robert McLachlan Wilson (San Francisco: Harper and Row, 1983) 211.

[27] Pagels, *The Gnostic Gospels*, 49.

[28] Bock, *Breaking the Da Vinci Code*, 76.

we are left with the traditional assessment, standard in antiquity, of the woman as a creature subordinated to man. . . . That this is the case is clear from certain evidence which regards a redemption of the woman as possible only on the condition of her metamorphosis into a man."[29] This is stated explicitly in the last line of the Gospel of Thomas: "Simon Peter said to them, 'Let Mary leave us, because women are not worthy of Life.' Jesus said, 'Look, I shall lead her so that I will make her male in order that she also may become a living spirit, resembling you males. For every woman who makes herself male will enter the kingdom of heaven.'" One finds a similar view even among the followers of Valentinus, one of whom said that a woman must become male to enter into the Pleroma.[30] And there are other examples.

If in much of the Gnostic literature women must renounce their physical identity and become "perfect men" to be accepted,[31] then the Gnostic exaltation of the sacred feminine or recognition of the equality of men and women is highly dubious. By contrast, the early Church in the person of Paul taught that the sexual union of husband and wife images Christ's union with the Church (Eph 5:32). Recently, feminist scholarship has helped us to recognize that the Church honored women as teachers, prophets, patrons, house-church leaders, missionaries, and perhaps apostles in the early New Testament period,[32] while the Church of the second and following centuries honored them as martyrs. Admittedly there was a loss of the more egalitarian ethos of the earliest days as the Church struggled for acceptance in patriarchal Greco-Roman society.

Jesus and Mary Magdalene

Do the Gnostic gospels suggest a sexual relationship between Jesus and Mary Magdalene? It's true that the Gospel of Philip (late third century) says "And the companion of [. . .] Mary Magdalene [. . . loved] her more than [all] the disciples [and used to] kiss her [often] on her [. . .]." There are many gaps in the manuscript, literally holes, so we don't know where this supposed kiss fell, on her mouth, feet, hand, or wherever. *The Da Vinci Code* argues that the Aramaic word *companion* in

[29] Rudolph, *Gnosis*, 271–72.
[30] Ibid., 272.
[31] Witherington, *The Gospel Code*, 90–92.
[32] See Eldon Jay Epp, *Junia: The First Woman Apostle* (Minneapolis: Fortress Press, 2005).

this text means *spouse*. Unfortunately, the text is written in Coptic, not Aramaic, and the Coptic word for companion, *koinonos*, is not a technical term for wife and in this literature is generally translated as "sister," in a spiritual sense.[33]

As Witherington notes, the context suggests that the kiss mentioned was most probably a chaste kiss of fellowship: "What makes this especially likely is that Philip is a Gnostic document, where human sexual expression is seen as defiling."[34] Thus, the idea of a sexual relationship between Jesus and Mary Magdalene is actually contrary to the whole ascetical spirit of Gnosticism, which saw the body and thus sexuality as belonging to the realm of matter. The Gnostics sought to escape all expression of the material which in most Gnostic traditions was seen as evil. As Witherington says, "The important point is that even this text doesn't clearly say or even suggest that Jesus was married at all, much less to Mary Magdalene."[35]

Aside from the fact that there is absolutely nothing in Christian literature or subsequent history that suggests that Jesus was married, what is for me the most convincing evidence comes from St. Paul, though admittedly it is an argument from silence. When defending his freedom as an apostle, Paul says "Do we not have the right to take along a Christian wife, as do the rest of the apostles, and the brothers of the Lord, and Kephas [Peter]" (1 Cor 9:5). If Jesus had been married, why doesn't Paul include him in his list? He was familiar with the teaching of Jesus, including his prohibition of divorce (1 Cor 7:10), yet he does not strengthen his argument by saying that Jesus too had a wife, for obvious reasons.

Could Jesus Have Had Children?

One of the more curious arguments in Brown's book is the notion that the Church had to suppress the story of Mary Magdalene and the bloodline that stemmed from her marriage to Jesus because it would threaten the Church's proclamation of his divinity (254). Think for a moment what Brown is suggesting. He's saying that if Jesus had been married and fathered a child, he could not have been divine, but only a mortal prophet. But this is to deny one of the Church's most basic doctrines, the true humanity of Jesus, reaffirmed by the Council of Chalcedon in 451.

---

[33] Witherington, *The Gospel Code*, 36–37.
[34] Ibid., 24.
[35] Ibid., 36.

Could Jesus have saved us if he had been married? Could he have had children? If he was truly human, the answer could only be of course. It has always fascinated me that the earliest heresy faced by the primitive Church was not a denial of the divinity of Jesus, but in fact, a denial of his humanity. As early as the end of the first century, some heterodox teachers were advocating a view known as Docetism, a form of Gnosticism that maintained that Jesus only "seemed" (Greek *dokeo*, to seem) to be human and thus, only seemed to die.

The heresy was typically Greek. To the dualist Greek mentality, the idea that the impassible, spiritual, divine could enter into the changing world of corruptible materiality, let alone take on flesh (*sarx*) with all its nastiness, was repugnant, and so they denied the humanity of Jesus. For example, in his polemic against the Gnostic Marcion, "On the Flesh of Christ," Tertullian argues against the Gnostic revulsion toward embodied, fleshly existence:

> So then, if it is neither as impossible nor as dangerous to God that you repudiate his becoming embodied, it remains for you to reject and denounce it on the ground that it was unworthy of him.
>
> Come, then, start from birth itself, the object of aversion, and run through your catalogue: the filth of the generative seeds within the womb, of the bodily fluid and the blood; the loathsome, curdled lump of flesh which has to be fed for nine months off this same muck.[36]

Here is the true face of Gnosticism and its offshoot, Docetism, with its distaste for the earthly, the material, and the human. The Church vigorously rejected Docetism, for it denied the reality of Christ's saving death as well as his presence in the Eucharist. Strangely, Brown never mentions the Church's struggle against Docetism. So how can he claim that the Church denied the humanity of Jesus?

Other Errors

There are other errors, misstatements, or simple falsehoods in Dan Brown's book—too many to mention. Let me try to point out just a few. According to Brown, "virtually all the elements of Catholic ritual—the

---

[36] Tertullian, *On the Flesh of the Christ*, 4,1; cited by Richard A. Norris, Jr. ed., *The Christological Controversy* (Philadelphia: Fortress, 1980) 67.

miter, the altar, the doxology and communion, the act of 'God-eating'—
were taken directly from earlier pagan mystery religions" (232). Much
too simple! It is true that much of the symbolism of the papal office, including the miter, the pallium and the title *Pontifex Maximus* or sovereign
pontiff, was borrowed from the Roman emperor as the Church became
enculturated in the Roman empire. The Eucharist has its roots in the
Jewish Passover Supper, the table fellowship tradition in the life of Jesus,
and his sharing bread and wine as symbols of his body broken and blood
poured out at the Last Supper. The altar of course was from Judaism,
though for the earliest Christians it was more properly a table.

Brown enlivens his text with just a hint of orgies, for example, the last
meeting of the Priory of Sion with Sophie's grandfather Dr. Jacques
Saunière presiding. But he also asserts that worship in the early Jewish
tradition involved ritual sex in the Temple (309). Never mind that the
early Israelite tradition did not have a Temple. What is true is that their
Canaanite neighbors practiced a seductive fertility cult, against which
the prophets of Israel continued to preach, forbidding intermarriage and
the religious syncretism to which it always led. When Brown says that
the Holy of Holies "housed not only God but also His powerful female
equal, Shekinah," he uses a word found not in the Bible, but only in the
later rabbinic writings. It means not a female consort, but God's nearness
to his people.

Even sillier is his assertion that the sacred *tetragrammaton*, the four
letters YHWH (remember that Hebrew was written without the vowels),
was "derived from Jehovah, an androgynous physical union between
the masculine *Jah* and the pre-Hebraic name for Eve, *Havah*" (309). Most
theology students know that the pronunciation "Jehovah," introduced
in the sixteenth century (to the embarrassment of the Jehovah Witnesses)
resulted from combining the consonants of YHWH with the superscripted
vowels from Adonai, reminding the synagogue reader not to pronounce
the sacred name but to substitute Adonai, "Lord." In other words, the
word Jehovah comes from a misreading of vowel points entered into the
ancient texts in the ninth or tenth century. The correct vocalization for
the holy name is most likely "Jahweh" or "Yahweh."

The idea that the Catholic Church is responsible for burning some
"five million women" for witchcraft is a slur still heard frequently today
(125). The actual history is far more complicated. A recent study by Ronald
Modras points out that the greatest number of witch trials took place, not
in the dark middle ages under the rule of the Church, but between 1550
and 1650, in other words, in early modernity, and that most were in the

hands of secular courts. Both Catholics and Protestants agreed about the danger of witches, and many of the hunts were the result of pressure from the masses, not the Church. The number of women killed is estimated today at 60,000, a horrible figure to be sure, but a far cry from the number given by Brown. Furthermore, most witch hunts took place in Germany, the British Isles, and Scandinavia, not in Catholic Italy and Spain.[37]

An interesting footnote is the fact that a German Jesuit, Friedrich Spee von Langfield (1591–1663) (a distant relative to the German admiral after whom the pocket battleship was named), spent years fighting against the persecution of these women. His book, *Cautio Criminalis*, played a major role in bringing an end to what Modras calls "a shameful conjunction of religious superstition and legally countenanced injustice."[38]

I won't attempt to analyze the artistic arguments the book presents; I refer the reader instead to the work by Carl Olson and Sandra Miesel, *The Da Vinci Hoax*, which devotes an entire chapter to them. But one must be addressed, at least briefly. One of Brown's principal arguments is that Leonardo de Vinci's famous painting, *The Last Supper*, pictures Mary Magdalene seated next to Jesus, rather than the traditional apostle John, or more accurately, the "Beloved Disciple," an argument that comes not from his research, but from *The Templar Revelation*.[39] Olson and Miesel cite a number of art critics, among them the well-known Leo Steinberg, author of *Leonardo's Incessant Last Supper*.[40] All identify the figure on Jesus' right as the apostle John.

Thus I've found no critics who have identified Mary Magdalene with the figure to the right of Jesus in Da Vinci's famous painting. This seems as much wishful thinking on Brown's part as his Sophie Neveu seeing in the figure to the right of Jesus "the hint of a bosom" (234).

Conclusion

What can we say in conclusion? To me, what makes a book like this objectionable is that so many confuse its fiction with history, particularly

[37] See Ronald Modras, "A Jesuit in the Crucible: Friedrich Spee and the Witchcraft Hysteria in Seventeenth Century Germany," *Studies in the Spirituality of Jesuits* 35/4 (2003) 6–9; see esp. Brian P. Levack, *The Witch-Hunt in Early Modern Europe* (London/ New York: Longman, 1987).

[38] Ibid., 35.

[39] Olson and Miesel, 263.

[40] New York: Zone Books, 2001.

those who are not very well-informed about the foundations of their faith. There's no question that the portrayals of God and the Church in popular culture can be challenging and confusing. That is why it is more important than ever to have an understanding of the faith and its history. Even though it can be difficult to sort through and negotiate some of these cultural spaces, doing so can be fruitful and enriching.

Some years ago I heard a popular song, sung by Joan Osborne and now used as the theme song for the TV show Joan of Arcadia.[41] At first I was startled by it, with its overstated, very anthropomorphic language. Then I realized how profoundly true it was. She sang:

> What if God was one of us?
> Just a slob like one of us
> Just a stranger on the bus
> Trying to make his way home.

Indeed, that is the central message of Christian faith, so offensive to many today just as it was to the Gnostics, that in Jesus God has taken on our flesh, shared our life, suffered, died, was raised up, and continues to dwell among us.

The next two chapters outline the important role of two central locations for Catholic formation, the Catholic home and Catholic schools, particularly Catholic colleges and universities.

[41] My thanks for this reference to Ben Witherington, *The Gospel Code*, 150.

Chapter 4

The Domestic Church

I usually begin my undergraduate theology classes by asking my students to write a religious autobiography. I ask them to describe their own personal religious journeys up to the present moment, suggesting the following points for reflection: how would you describe your own religious or church background and particular faith stance? Were there some key moments or experiences that have brought you to where you are today? What informs your own religious identity or religious imagination? What people and events have contributed to your current religious attitudes and theological understanding? How has your home been an influence? Where have you experienced God? How would you describe your image of God at this point in your life, and has it changed from earlier days?

The assignment is helpful for a number of reasons. First of all, it encourages the students to reflect on their own religious experience at the very beginning of the semester. Second, it helps me to get to know them in a more personal way, to get a sense for the ecclesial and faith traditions present in the class, and to have a sense for where each student is as an individual. Finally, it often surfaces issues that will be good to take up later in the class. I tell them the assignment is personal and confidential; I won't "grade" it or reveal what they tell me, but it will help me to gain a sense for who the students are that I will be spending the semester with. I find most of them candid in telling their stories, and often very insightful. Having done this for years now, it has brought a number of things home to me that are particularly important in the developing faith and religious identity of a young adult.

Perhaps the one thing that emerges with utter clarity is how influential parents and family are in handing on the faith. Many of those who come to the university practicing their faith come with their parents' faith; of course many are no longer practicing. In both cases, a milestone in their religious journeys will be discovering their own faith, and many of them do during their days at the university. But those who come with a strong, personally appropriated religious identity, particularly a strong Catholic identity, almost always come from homes where that faith has been lived, cherished, and expressed by significant members of their families, particularly their parents, in stories, customs, rituals, and practices.

Handing on the Faith

The UNC study on youth and religion argues that the lower levels of church attendance between Catholic and Protestant teenagers "can be significantly explained" by the "lower levels of religiosity" of the Catholic teens' parents.[1] These differences were so significant that the investigators devoted a separate chapter to the lower levels of religiosity found among Catholic teens. Even with controls for variables factored in, the study indicated that "the relative religious laxity of most U.S. Catholic teenagers significantly reflects the relative religious laxity of their parents" (216–17). The parents surveyed were less likely to attend church regularly, more likely to attend infrequently or never, less likely to participate in other parish-based activities than the parents of Protestant teenagers, less likely to say that their faith is "extremely or very important" in their lives or to be married to someone of the same faith (209). The study suggests that Catholic dioceses and parishes need to devote more resources to youth ministry and education (210, 214).

Similarly, the young adult Catholics surveyed by Hoge and his colleagues generally gave a low grade to the Church for its efforts in religious education.[2] Their findings generally substantiated the common assumption that "when individuals come from stable families in which both parents were practicing Catholics and committed church members, they tend to remain Catholics as adults, even when they have periods of church inactivity in late adolescence, or when they reject doctrines and forms of piety and devotionalism practiced by their parents."[3]

---

[1] Christian Smith and Melinda Lundquist Denton, *Soul Searching: The Religious and Spiritual Lives of American Teenagers* (New York: Oxford University Press, 2005) 210.

[2] Dean R. Hoge, William D. Dinges, Mary Johnson, Juan L. Gonzales, Jr., *Young Adult Catholics: Religion in the Culture of Choice* (Notre Dame, IN: University of Notre Dame Press, 2001) 148.

[3] Ibid., 158.

The influence of parents and family is especially true of students from ethnic backgrounds strongly rooted in a Catholic culture, Mexican and Filipino Americans in particular. Often they will tell stories of domestic rituals or expressions of popular religion that have made the stories of their Catholic faith a part of their own personal identity. In their study of young adult Catholics, Dean Hoge, et al., note that Latino Catholics were more involved in personal devotions, including making the Stations of the Cross, praying the rosary, wearing medals and scapulars, having images of the saints in the home or having their cars blessed, more engaged in prayer groups, faith sharing, novenas, and other spiritual healing groups.[4] In theological terms, these young people with significant levels of religious practice are those who have been formed by a domestic church, a term used since Christianity's earliest days.

The Church in the Home

The earliest Christians gathered for teaching (*didachē*), preaching (*kerygma*), fellowship (*koinōnia*), worship (*leitourgia*), and ministry (*diakonia*) in the homes of one of the members of the community, probably one prosperous enough to have a house that could accommodate the community. St. Paul frequently refers to these house churches or "church at their house" in his epistles (1 Cor 16:19; Rom 16:5; Col 4:15). This domestic setting is evidence that church itself is not a temple, a building, or some other holy place, but the gathering of Christians together; it is an assembly of the faithful. Indeed, the conversion of a household or family was often the beginning of a local church (cf. Acts 11:14; 16:31; 18:8). Paul speaks of the love of husband and wife for each other as a symbol (*mysterion*) of Christ's love for the Church (Eph 5:32), using the word Greek *mysterion* which would be later translated by the Latin *sacramentum*.

The Second Vatican Council speaks of the family as a domestic church (*ecclesia domestica*) (LG 11). The phrase has a long history, going back to John Chrysostom in the fourth century who spoke of the family as a little church (*micra ecclesia*) and Augustine who called it a domestic church (*domestica ecclesia*). In a real sense, Vatican II recovered this concept, reinserting the concept of the domestic church into modern theological

---

[4] Ibid., 118.

language.[5] Pope John Paul II frequently spoke of the family as the domestic church, particularly in his Apostolic Constitution, *Familiaris consortio*, in which he roots its ecclesial status in both word and sacrament:

> A vivid and attentive awareness of the mission that they have received with the sacrament of marriage will help Christian parents to place themselves at the service of their children's education with great serenity and trustfulness, and also with a sense of responsibility before God, who calls them and gives them the mission of building up the Church in their children. Thus in the case of baptized people, the family, called together by word and sacrament as the Church of the home, is both teacher and mother, the same as the worldwide Church (no. 38).

In the Eastern Church, which sees an analogy between priestly ordination and marriage, the bride and groom are crowned in the marriage ceremony as a sign of their share in the priesthood of Christ.

The *Catechism of the Catholic Church* also develops the idea of the family as the domestic church. Just as the Church is "the family of God" (1655), in our modern world, often hostile to faith, "believing families are of primary importance as centers of living faith" (1656).

> It is here that the father of the family, the mother, children, and all members of the family exercise the *priesthood of the baptized* in a privileged way 'by the reception of the sacraments, prayer and thanksgiving, the witness of a holy life, and self-denial and active charity.' Thus the home is the first school of Christian life and 'a school for human enrichment.' Here one learns endurance and the joy of work, fraternal love, generous—even repeated—forgiveness, and above all divine worship in prayer and the offering of one's life (1657).

With its deep roots in the Christian tradition and the place it occupies in the teaching of Pope John Paul II and the *Catechism*, it is regrettable that so few Catholics think of the Catholic family as a domestic church. More traditional Catholics show a great appreciation for the concept; there are numerous websites celebrating the domestic church with many

---

[5] See Joseph C. Atkinson, "Family as Domestic Church: Developmental Trajectory, Legitimacy, and Problems of Appropriation," *Theological Studies* 66 (2005) 592.

practical ideas. An especially good source is Florence Caffrey Bourg's book on the subject, which is concerned to address what she calls "the doctrinal vacuum surrounding domestic church." She approaches it from the perspectives of sacramental ecclesiology, Aquinas' teaching on virtue, and a consistent life ethic.[6]

While growing up in a home in which both parents are present does not assure that the children will be psychologically well-adjusted, self-confident, and moral, there is increasing evidence that children from homes with absent parents or other forms of parent-child separation are at considerable disadvantage. Mary Eberstadt charts this relentlessly, from the problems of day care to children who are angry, suicidal, fat, overmedicated, sexually active, afflicted with sexually transmitted diseases, or "outsourced" in specialty boarding schools. If life is better for their parents, who are more free in so many respects, "life is *not* better for many American children, no matter how many extra Game Boys they have, no matter how much more pocket money they have for the vending machines, and no matter how nice it is that Dad's new wife gave them their own weekend bedroom in his new place."[7]

The ecclesial dimensions of a genuinely Christian family life are unmistakable. If young Catholics today grow up without the Catholic subculture that gave Catholics of another generation a clear sense of who they were, it becomes all the more important to find effective ways to introduce them to the stories and traditions of their faith. It is also true that not every Catholic family realizes the Church's ideal vision of marriage. Reviewing the challenges faced by those in canonically invalid marriages, interchurch families, and single parent families, Bourg is cautious about ranking some families as "more Christian" than others and suggests that baptism (rather than marriage) should be considered the domestic church's primary sacrament.[8] Thomas Groome, noting that most families are not perfect, argues that "we need to shift our imaginations beyond the nuclear family of a mom, dad, and two kids, include extended and blended families, single-, double-, and triple-parent families,

---

[6] Florence Caffrey Bourg, *Where Two or Three are Gathered: Christian Families as Domestic Churches* (Notre Dame, Indiana: University of Notre Dame Press, 2004) 157.

[7] See Mary Eberstadt, *Home-alone America: the Hidden Toll of Day Care, Behavioral Drugs, and other Parent Substitutes* (New York: Sentinel, 2004); also Brad Wilcox, *Soft Patriarchs, New Men: How Christianity Shapes Husbands and Fathers* (University of Chicago Press, 2004) xvi.

[8] Bourg, *Where Two or Three Are Gathered*, 69–80.

straight, gay, and bent families. Family is any bonded network of domestic life and nurture."[9]

Joseph Atkinson argues against a "non-objective approach" that would see the domestic church as a "concept" into which one pours one's own "content," denying that the Christian faith transforms a family, giving it a new ontological reality.[10] Bourg's approach seems to stress the importance of a Christian intentionality, rooted in baptism into Christ, while Atkinson, though also stressing baptism, seems to move beyond intentionality to sacramental marriage as a sign of contradiction: "When, in love, we give ourselves bodily to another in covenantal terms, our two bodies become one flesh in Christ, the fruit of which is the procreation of other bodily realities made in the image of God."[11] But in the end a question remains. If Atkinson implies sacramental marriage as the basis for the domestic church, he does not say so explicitly. He does say that to be in Christ means "to seek to be formed by and in him not as an ideal but in our own actual historical reality."

Is there a way beyond this impasse? The Catholic Church recognizes the marriage of a baptized man and woman as sacrament; that is to say, God's grace is here, made visible in their union with and love for each other, in their love for their children who are the expression of that love, and in their love for the Church. It cannot make the same affirmation about nontraditional families.

At the same time, Karl Rahner has emphasized that grace transcends even the sacraments.[12] He states, "Grace, justification, and even unity with the Body of Christ in his Spirit (the *res sacramenti* in the Eucharist) are in fact possible and become a reality even apart from baptism, the sacrament of penance, and the Eucharist."[13] Catholic theology recognizes that the grace of the sacrament can be present at times outside of the sacrament; God's grace is not limited by the Church's sacramental and canonical discipline. It would be difficult to deny that a nontraditional union, in which the partners love each other and their children with a life-giving and self-sacrificing love, may indeed be an effective sign of

---

[9] Thomas Groome, "Good Governance, the Domestic Church, and Religious Education," in *Common Calling: The Laity and Governance of the Catholic Church*, ed. Stephen J. Pope (Washington, D.C.: Georgetown University Press, 2004) 203–04.

[10] Joseph Atkinson, "Family as Domestic Church," 603.

[11] Ibid., 604.

[12] Karl Rahner, *The Dynamic Element in the Church* (New York: Herder and Herder, 1964).

[13] Rahner, *Theological Investigations* 12 (New York: Seabury Press, 1974) 48.

the grace of the sacrament, even if the Church cannot officially recognize it as such.

Expressions of the Domestic Church

If Church is a Christian community expressed through preaching, teaching, fellowship, ministry, and worship, how are these expressions of Church realized in the Christian family, the domestic church. For children and young adults, it is first of all in the home that the Gospel is heard and understood and Christian stories are learned, not just in Scripture, but also the stories of the saints and great figures in the tradition. Religious art symbolizes a family's faith commitment. Prayer and domestic rituals enact it and sacraments celebrate it. Let's consider some of these elements.

Story

Andrew Greeley's repeated emphasis on the formative value of stories is a point well made. He stresses that a religious sensibility is passed on most effectively by storytelling, in a way that the storyteller is often unaware because who the person is and what the person does is more important that what he or she says. Citing his study of young Catholics, he says that "the Catholic sensibility is passed on first through the stories one hears at the dawn of consciousness and that slip, via images and pictures (the Madonna, the crèche), subtly into that consciousness during the early years of life."[14] Significant "socializing influences," particularly parents and spouses, but also siblings, relatives, friends, the parish community, the liturgy—all reinforce and add layers of religious influence.[15] Particularly important is the father's involvement in the religious life and practice of the family since children generally expect their mothers to be religious.

A study published in Switzerland (2000) indicated that if both parents attended church regularly, 33 percent of their children would end up as regular churchgoers and 41 percent would attend irregularly. Only a quarter will not practice at all. Perhaps most important was the finding

---

[14] Andrew M. Greeley, *The Catholic Imagination* (Berkeley: University of California Press, 2000) 175.

[15] Ibid., 175–76.

that if the mother practices and the father does not, only 2 percent of the children will become regular worshippers, while 37 percent will practice irregularly. But 60 percent will be lost to the church.[16]

When I recall my own memories of growing up in a Catholic home, the example of my parents was primary. Sunday Mass was a family event, as was breakfast afterward. I also remember my parents rising early to go to morning Mass on weekdays and Saturdays. We learned to "offer up" our little pains and frustrations for hungry children and victims of disasters and sensed that we were participating in some way in the cross of Jesus. Without being particularly pious, we had cherished religious symbols at home. I remember a Madonna on a table in the living room and a triptych on the hall table. To this day I remember our annual Christmas project of making clay figures for a crèche we would put on the mantle. One of us made a figure with a halo that kept falling off, christened "St. Collapsible." I recall my mother interrupting the excitement of playing with the gifts under the Christmas tree on a Christmas morning, to gather us before the crèche and say some prayers, reminding us what that morning was really all about.

I still remember the stories the sisters in grammar school used to tell us after the lunch hour before we resumed classes, stories of the terrible sufferings of St. Isaac Jogues and his companions, about St. Tarcisius, a twelve-year-old acolyte in third century Rome who was attacked by a pagan mob while he was carrying the blessed sacrament and died trying to protect it, of St. Dominic Savio (d. 1857), patron of the falsely accused, stepping between two boys engaged in a vicious rock fight with his crucifix, and about St. Thérèse, the Little Flower, whose statue in the church showed her showering down roses on those who prayed to her. We also would look forward to receiving a copy of *Treasure Chest*, a Catholic comic books series distributed only through the Catholic school system. We read the stories about Chuck White and his friends, and another about Eugenio Pacelli, later Pope Pius XII, as a young papal representative in Munich, facing down Communist demonstrators who were threatening him in his residence. Today those of my generation often laugh at those stories. They were certainly pious and sometimes exaggerated. But they not only fired out imaginations; they told us who

---

[16] Werner Haug and Phillipe Warner, ed., *The Demographic Characteristics of National Minorities in Certain European States* (Strasbourg: Council of Europe Directorate General III, Social Cohesion, January 2000); cited by Robbie Low, "The Truth about Men and Church," *Touchstone* 16/5 (June 2003).

we were as Catholic Christians and how to express our faith in difficult situations in our lives.

What is so regrettable is that most young Catholics do not know stories like these anymore. Nor are they very familiar with everyday events in the life of the contemporary Church. When I ask my students what Catholic journals, magazines, or newspapers their families subscribe to, they look at me in confusion. Few would be able to name any, except perhaps the *Catholic Digest* and occasionally the diocesan newspaper. Most have never heard of *America, Commonweal,* the *National Catholic Reporter* or the *National Catholic Register.* When I give them an assignment that requires them to report on a controversial issue in the church, using several Catholic magazines or newspapers, they are unable to identify the viewpoints in the sources they consult, whether far left or far right, as they are so unfamiliar with various points of view.

As an educated community, most Catholics take it for granted that they need to continue to read and study in their chosen fields. But the sorry fact is that most adult Catholics today read very little to keep themselves current in their faith, and so have little to pass on to their children. And how many parents take the time to read to their children before they retire? This is a wonderful tradition, and offers an opportunity to rehearse some of the stories of the faith.

How many children know the stories of the saints for whom they are named? Unfortunately, today an increasing number of children have secular names rather than the name of a saint. In Africa a convert usually receives a new name that expresses some aspect of the faith he or she has now embraced. How many families still have in their homes the *Maryknoll* magazine which I've read since I was ten, with its stories of Catholic missionary and evangelical work around the world?

Not so long ago I was moved by a conversation with a young friend of mine who was expecting her first child. She and her husband, both successful attorneys, are already taking steps that their child become familiar with the stories of their faith. Her husband, having sought out several children's books on the saints, reads to their unborn child almost every night in bed—currently the story of Francis of Assisi. His wife tells me that she can feel the child responding, and that it does not move within her in the same way on those nights he is not able to continue his reading. Another friend told me that when his children were young he and his wife would read to them at the end of each day a story from Robert Ellsberg's *All Saints,* a marvelous book which offers a reflection on a different saint, prophetic figure, or heroic Christian for each day of the year. Each mini-story provides a sketch of the person's life and brief summary of his or her spirituality.[17]

Religious Symbol

In another generation, Catholic homes were rich in religious symbols. Crucifixes in each room, often a holy water stoup in a bedroom, a picture of the Sacred Heart or the Good Shepherd, a Madonna or other Marian symbol, sometimes a domestic shrine with a vigil light or candle, a family Bible in which births and deaths were recorded, Last Supper scenes in the dining room. Blessed palms from Palm Sunday were kept through the year, often behind a crucifix or icon. Children received prayer books, rosaries, and crucifixes for First Communion and other religious events, wore scapulars or religious medals, marked their places in their books with holy cards, and had pictures in their bedrooms to remind them of their guardian angels. Granted, the quality of many of these symbols was more kitsch than art; today we are embarrassed by blue-eyed pictures of Jesus and dolorous representations of the Sacred Heart or otherworldly Madonnas.

But what has taken the place of these symbols in the contemporary Catholic home? Is it the television set that centers the family room? Is the crucifix displayed prominently and the Bible in a place of honor? Is there any good religious art, an icon or hand-carved image of Mary or a saint? Do children have religious objects they can learn to cherish?

Prayer

Children's first ideas about God come from their parents, and from them they learn how to pray. The Catholic tradition has a rich tradition of prayer, though many Catholics are unfamiliar with it today.[18] Teaching a small child the Sign of the Cross, the Our Father, Hail Mary, Hail Holy Queen, the Doxology or Glory Be to the Father offers precious opportunities for sharing one's own faith with one's children. The Morning Offering is still a very meaningful prayer, teaching a child to consecrate the day to God in communion with the universal Church. I've heard

---

[17] Robert Ellsberg, *All Saints: Daily Reflections on Saints, Prophets, and Witnesses for our Time* (New York: Crossroad, 1997).

[18] See Edward Hays, *Prayers for the Domestic Church: A Handbook for Worship in the Home* (Notre Dame, IN: Ave Maria Press, 1989).

parents complain that their children didn't learn traditional prayers in Catholic school or CCD programs. Some parents used to blame the nuns, or today the religious educators. But their very protest about what their children have not learned always indicates that they themselves have not taught them how to pray. As Thomas Groome says, "Even while participating in the formal programs of a parish, every Christian should be 'home-schooled' in their faith."[19]

A friend of mine who teaches in a Catholic high school discovered that most of her students had never participated in a May Crowning. So she developed one, to honor not just Mary the Mother of Jesus but all the women who had blessed their lives and served as models. It was a great success. The pastor came to each class and loved it. Many young adults don't know how to pray the rosary. Several times in my Christian Life Community meetings (a small faith-sharing group that gathers for community, spirituality, and service, based on the Ignatian tradition), a student has introduced the rosary, bringing rosaries for the members of the group and teaching them how to pray it.

Many Catholics today are more comfortable with spontaneous prayer, something else that can be learned at home. "Grace" before meals is an opportunity for this kind of prayer, though this is made more difficult today because so few families, given the often chaotic character of modern family life, have time to dine together. Other opportunities might include praying the rosary together, reading from the Bible, or bedtime prayers with the younger children. Such moments easily become a kind of domestic liturgy.

Domestic Rituals

If the home is a domestic church, then there should be rituals that express the family's participation in the Church's liturgical cycle. Making an Advent wreath and lighting it to initiate the Advent season, marking the days with an Advent card, those wonderful cards with all the little doors that used to enthrall my younger brother, a sign of Advent expectation and hope, making sure that there is a crib or crèche under the Christmas tree, celebrating Candlemas, the Feast of the Presentation with a special beeswax candle, fasting during Lent, draping the domestic crucifix with Lenten purple, or placing flowers before a statue of Mary

---

[19] Thomas Groome, "Good Governance, the Domestic Church, and Religious Education," 206.

during May. Because Catholic time is liturgical, it is sacred time. December is the season of Advent, May the month of our Lady, October the rosary, and November a time to remember the holy souls. Other family rituals might include recognizing family members' patron saints' feast days, often the custom in Europe, or adopting a particular charity that the family makes its own.

I have always been impressed by how students from strong Catholic ethnic cultures have been shaped by their domestic rituals. Mexican Americans celebrate Our Lady of Guadalupe, though I've met Chicano students who no longer know the story of Juan Diego and the Virgin; Christmas is a time for *Las Posadas*, a custom of going door to door with candlelight processions for nine consecutive nights, beginning December 16, asking for shelter for the holy family. Another popular celebration is a *Quinceanera*, a celebration of a girl's fifteenth birthday. Though they can often add a great financial burden to a poor family, when done properly, it can become an important occasion marking her transition from childhood to being a woman. Richard Rohr argues that the lack of such rites of passage for young males inhibits their learning how to enter society as responsible adults.[20]

One of my students described a domestic ritual practiced in his home: "when a friend or family member passes away my mother places a candle and a dish full of food for that person for the next three days, with a new dish each day. The reasoning behind this is that the person needs to feel remembered as he or she transcends into the next world." Another described a domestic shrine, "a corner of my house where there's a shrine dedicated to relatives who have died with a large candle, photos, and holy cards surrounding each picture."

Filipinos also have their own domestic rituals; in one of them, a statue of Mary is brought to a particular home in the community and kept there for a week or two, while the family and their neighbors gather together for prayer and devotion. With their strong emphasis on the family, a baptism or First Communion becomes the occasion for a great family celebration, with much food and dancing. Such domestic rituals can also help break down the clerical dominance so typical of Catholicism.

These domestic rituals are expressions of a popular religiosity, often misunderstood by non-Catholics, but tolerated and generally encouraged by the Church as ways of enculturating the faith, giving it expression in

---

[20] Richard Rohr, *Adam's Return: The Five Promises of Male Initiation* (New York: Crossroad, 2004).

the traditions and iconography of a people. Devotion to Our Lady of Guadalupe is an example of this, but European Catholicism has also incorporated many such celebrations of popular culture, from the Christmas tree to the Maypole, though the origins of most of them are no longer remembered.

Sacraments

Bourg argues that the family itself is sacramental. Using the work of Rahner, she contrasts the position that God is encountered primarily in the sacred realm—the Church and its sacraments, to construct a theology that envisions the so-called secular world as permeated by God's grace. From this perspective, the family as the domestic church becomes "the forum where the Church as sacrament does its most basic work."[21] In all their activities, ordinary and extraordinary, domestic churches can cultivate a sacramental vision among their members, manifesting God's presence. They are not however self-sufficient; each needs God's working through the larger Church, including other households, to nurture a sacramental perspective.[22]

In a wonderful, very personal example, Bourg relates how at a moment of particular stress she had to miss the Holy Thursday liturgy because she had to care for a sick child. While cleaning him, somewhat resentfully, for what seemed like the hundredth time, she found herself washing his feet, only to realize in a flash of inspiration that she was celebrating in her own way the Gospel message (John 13) of the missed liturgy, with its beautiful enactment of Jesus washing the feet of his disciples. And so domestic chore became sacrament.[23]

It is the larger Church that makes explicit God's presence sacramentally in the world—and we might add—in family life. The attitudes toward the sacramental life of the Church are formed in the home, often indelibly. Students in their religious autobiographies will write of going to church with their parents, of sitting uncomprehending in the pews, or wanting to receive Communion, or of being bored, but they will also mention something a parent said to them that "stuck" about the Eucharist or worship or prayer. They read right away what is being said when parents insist that they go to church, but don't go themselves. Discussing the

---

[21] Bourg, *Where Two or Three Are Gathered*, 97.
[22] Ibid., 107.
[23] Ibid., 133.

homily at the Sunday breakfast table sometimes brings home the message, and personalizes it, because it is now expressed in terms that a child can understand.

Two events that students mention repeatedly as especially significant in their autobiographies are high school *Kairos* retreats, and Confirmation. Some will acknowledge that they were confirmed due to parental pressure, but for many others it was the first time that they made a real decision for the practice of their faith themselves. Some choose not to be confirmed, wanting to do it when it was their decision, not someone else's. Families have an important role to play here. Parents communicate attitudes toward sacraments in the life of a young person, but also have to respect his or her freedom and personal faith journey, something that calls on the deepest sources of their parental wisdom.

Conclusion

Writing this has brought me to reflect considerably on my own education in the faith. While there were many influences, not the least the schools I attended, certainly my home played the most important part. This was confirmed by the UNC study. As the authors emphasize, the best rule of thumb for adults considering the possible "faith outcome" of their children is, "We'll get what we are."[24] They believe that "the evidence clearly shows that single most important social influence on the religious and spiritual lives of adolescents is their parents."[25] But this should not be a surprise. The idea of the family as a domestic church is deeply rooted in the Catholic tradition and has been stressed again by Vatican II and Pope John Paul II. The family is the cradle of faith, the hearth at which it is warmed and nurtured in story and symbol, prayer and domestic rituals, and sacramental celebrations.

But how many Catholics couples today see the ecclesial dimensions of their sacrament of matrimony. How many see their home as a domestic church? Certainly more traditional Catholics do. There are innumerable websites on the domestic church available, with both theological commentary and concrete ideas for bringing it to practical, affective expression. Much of it less traditional Catholics might find too pious, archaic, even embarrassing.

---

[24] Smith and Denton, *Soul Searching*, 216.
[25] Ibid., 261.

Still I wonder if we haven't made our faith too much something of the head, too abstract, theological but not speaking to the affective side of ourselves. Robert Barron speaks of growing up in the "beige" Catholicism of the sixties and seventies, and continues to object to "beige churches, that is to say, structures that are largely void of symbolism, imagery, iconography, and narrativity."[26] I wonder if this couldn't also describe the Catholic culture, or lack of it really, of many contemporary Catholic families.

To grow up without an appreciation for symbol and image, icon and story is to grow up without a Catholic imagination. It is to grow up without one's patrimony, a rich inheritance. Beige Catholicism is not just dull; it's essentially impoverished. A domestic church should be a rainbow of color.

[26] Robert Barron, *Bridging the Great divide: Musings of a Post-Liberal, Post-Conservative Evangelical Catholic* (Lanham, MD: Rowman & Littlefield Publishers, 2004) 269.

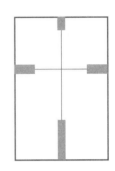

Chapter 5

Catholic Colleges and Universities

Among other Catholic institutions like hospitals and social service agencies such as Catholic Charities, the network of Catholic colleges and universities in the United States—some 238 institutions—is unique in the Church. Most of these schools, founded and directed by religious congregations, played an important role in educating an originally immigrant Catholic population. Particularly after the Second World War, when the GI Bill made it possible for returning Catholic veterans to gain college degrees, Catholic colleges and universities played a major role in making the Catholic community one of the most educated in the U.S.

In the years since the Second Vatican Council, most of these institutions have gone through a process of professionalization, rethinking their programs and curriculums, hiring professionally trained faculty, and putting a new emphasis on research and scholarship, sometimes at the cost of their Catholic identity. This "mainstreaming" of Catholic higher education has generally been successful. However, recent years have also seen the development or founding of a number of neoconservative Catholic institutions which, in reaction to what they see as the secular model followed by most Catholic universities, define their institutions as self-consciously Catholic, with an emphasis on fidelity to the papal magisterium, loyalty oaths for the faculty, and a narrowly understood orthodoxy. They include the Franciscan University of Steubenville (Ohio), Christendom College (Front Royal, Virginia), Thomas Aquinas College (Santa Paula, California), and most recently, Ave Maria University (Naples, Florida).

At the same time, mainstream Catholic institutions have begun showing a new concern for their Catholic identity, as has the official Church. In this chapter we will consider the professionalization of Catholic higher education, the apostolic letter of Pope John Paul II on Catholic identity, *Ex Corde Ecclesiae*, Catholic departments of theology and religious studies, and various steps Catholic colleges and universities are taking to safeguard and enhance their Catholic identity.

The Process of Professionalization

Catholic colleges and universities have traditionally placed a high priority on handing on the faith. Their faculties were largely Catholic, mostly priests and religious; they had heavy teaching loads, were generally under compensated, and not expected to publish. Academic rank generally reflected years of service, not scholarship. Students took a heavy dose of courses in philosophy and "religion," particularly in Jesuit institutions. John Haughey describes their "custodial" mode of operation: "Philosophy was taught with a view to making students effective apologists of the faith. Morality was largely of an individualistic, 'save one's soul' character. Religious education was to mature a presumed faith."[1]

These institutions began to change however in the years after the Second Vatican Council. As they sought to implement the more inclusive vision of the council and bring the laity into full partnership, they restructured their core curriculums, began hiring for professional competence, and moved deliberately away from the *"in loco parentis"* model of student life. The university's mission was increasingly understood as the intellectual rather than moral formation of its students. The challenge, of course, was how to be both Catholic and a genuine university.

An important step was taken July 1967 when a small group of Catholic educators, mostly priests, met at Land O'Lakes, Wisconsin, for a conference on how Catholic colleges and universities might participate in the renewal of the Church begun by the Second Vatican Council. In response, the majority of the schools began moving in the early seventies toward separate incorporation.[2] This meant bringing lay men and women on to their boards of trustees as equal members with religious, so that real

---

[1] John C. Haughey, "Theology and the Mission of the Jesuit College and University," *Conversations* 5 (Spring 1994) 5.

[2] See the "Land O'Lakes Statement: The Nature of a Catholic University," in *American Catholic Higher Education: Essential Documents, 1967–1990,* ed. Alice Gallin (Notre Dame, 1992).

control for the ordinary business of the schools rested with the trustees, not with the Church or sponsoring religious community. Thus they became church-related rather than canonically Catholic. At least one school, Fordham University, deliberately secularized its articles of incorporation, in order to be eligible for state aid. As Catholic universities began to professionalize, their academic reputations were enhanced; some became first rate. But the gain in academic standing was not without an overall loss to their religious identities.

By the 1990s, Catholic college and university administrators and faculty had begun expressing concern about this issue.[3] Some thought that it was already too late. With diminished numbers of religious men and women on campus, their faculties now looked as tweedy and as secular as their peers at other, non-Catholic institutions. Few administrators had any idea of how many of their faculty members were Catholics, and many who were no longer practiced their faith. Theology and philosophy requirements had been reduced, from a virtual double major in the Jesuit schools, to an average of two courses each.

Student life had changed enormously. Some resident facilities became coeducational, and students could visit each other's rooms at any hour of the day or night. Faculties were increasingly recognized for their scholarship, with many of the younger ones coming from non-Catholic graduate schools, many of which had little sympathy for the Catholic tradition. As John Langan points out, many of these faculty members came to feel very much at home in their new universities, yet tended to remain on the secular side of the culture wars. Reflecting the liberal academic culture from which they came, they generally accept abortion as a woman's right, support gay rights, and are reticent about expressing personal religious beliefs or backgrounds. While they often formed friendships with the religious among their colleagues, they remain suspicious of the Church or of Catholics in general.[4] Today, for example, many faculty members are comfortable with an institution's Jesuit tradition, but much more nervous about efforts to enhance its Catholic identity.

As the century drew to a close it had become clear to many that the religious identity of an institution was not a given. Many Catholic educators were familiar with George Marsden's book, *The Soul of the American*

---

[3] Steinfels, "Catholic Institutions and Catholic Identity," in his *A People Adrift* (New York: Simon and Schuster, 2003) 103–61.

[4] John Langan, "Reforging Catholic Identity: Will Non-Catholic Faculty Fit In?" *Commonweal* 127/8 (April 21, 2000) 21.

University: From Protestant Establishment to Established Nonbelief, which traced the way that many of the finest institutions of higher learning in the country, founded as Protestant schools, went through a process of alienation from their religious roots and ultimately became secular. Among them were Harvard, Yale, Princeton, Dartmouth, Wellesley, Vassar, Smith, Chicago, Stanford, and the University of Southern California. As Marsden argues, their insistence on moving beyond denominational or "confessional" identities to a "nonsectarian" religious universalism contributed ultimately "to the virtual exclusion of religious perspectives from the most influential centers of American intellectual life."[5]

Those at Catholic colleges and universities have had the history of their Protestant counterparts very much in mind. The last ten to fifteen years have seen considerable effort on the part of both Catholic educators and the official Catholic Church to address this issue. Catholic colleges and universities began appointing administrators in the late 1980s charged with caring for the mission and identity of the institution, setting up committees to address the issue, and holding workshops for faculty and staff. As William Portier observes, after the collapse of the Catholic subculture, "Catholic identity is the central issue."[6] In an address to about fifty university presidents and more than four hundred educators and administrators from Catholic colleges and universities, *New York Times'* correspondent Peter Steinfels spoke of an emerging consensus relating to what Catholic identity meant and the steps necessary to ensure it.[7] By this time Pope John Paul II had already addressed the issue in his 1990 apostolic letter *Ex Corde Ecclesiae*, "From the Heart of the Church."[8]

Ex Corde Ecclesiae

The Pope's letter has generally been welcomed for its call to Catholic educators to renew the Catholic identity of their institutions. He stressed that a Catholic university, born "from the heart of the church," is part of

---

[5] George Marsden, *The Soul of the American University: From Protestant Establishment to Established Nonbelief* (New York: Oxford University Press, 1994) 5.

[6] William L. Portier, "Here Come the Evangelical Catholics," *Communio* 31 (Spring 2004) 54.

[7] Peter Steinfels, "Catholic Identity: Emerging Consensus," *Origins* 25/11 (1995) 173–77.

[8] John Paul II, *Ex Corde Ecclesiae, Origins* 20/17 (1990) 265–76.

a tradition that may be traced back to the very origin of the university as an institution (no. 1). In a Catholic university, "research necessarily includes (a) the search for an integration of knowledge, (b) a dialogue between faith and reason, (c) an ethical concern and (d) a theological perspective" (no. 15). Its basic academic activities, its teaching, scholarship, professional training, and service should be "connected with and in harmony with the evangelizing mission of the Church" (no. 49).

Still, there has been considerable controversy over just how a university's Catholic identity could best be preserved and fostered. Like other institutions of higher learning, Catholic colleges and universities value their institutional autonomy and their freedom of inquiry. They are nervous about what might be seen as attempts to close off debate on controversial issues by administrators or Church officials. Who speaks on campus, what controversial questions can be raised, which student organizations are to be recognized—all these are questions which gray the hair of administrators. For others, even asking the question of Catholic identity is like raising a red flag. They fear a return to ecclesiastical control, or worry that non-Catholic faculty members will feel less welcome.

At the same time, many on Catholic campuses are now aware that some steps need to be taken to preserve and enhance the religious identity of their schools. How to do that effectively is the question. American educators prefer consultation and dialogue; Rome wants ordinances. In 1996 the National Council of Catholic Bishops approved a document in response to *Ex Corde* based on consultative procedures rather than juridical ones by a vote of 224 to 6. But it was rejected by Rome, which insisted on the inclusion of juridical elements. A more juridical text was then developed by a subcommittee of canonists chaired by Cardinal Anthony Bevilacqua of Philadelphia. It required that the university president make a profession of faith and take an oath of fidelity on assuming office; it also said that the majority of the members of the faculty and board of trustees should be "faithful Catholics."[9] Most Catholic educators found this language unacceptable, and their non-Catholic colleagues felt threatened, as though they were unwelcome.

After considerable reaction from both bishops and educators, a subsequent text (1999) softened its predecessor's language by adding a host of qualifying phrases and "shoulds." The majority of the board and faculty should be Catholic "to the extent possible." Rather than asking that

---

[9] "*Ex Corde Ecclesiae*: An Application to the United States," *Origins* 28/25 (1998) 438–44.

they be "faithful Catholics," they are to be "committed to the church" or to "the witness of the faith."[10] The requirement for a profession of faith on the part of the president was relegated to a footnote. It was this text that the bishops voted to implement.

The most controversial of the ordinances remains the requirement, in accordance with canon 812 of the 1983 Code of Canon Law, that Catholics who teach theological disciplines in Catholic higher educational institutions seek a *mandatum* from "competent ecclesiastical authority," that is, the bishop or his delegate. It is this requirement that is most problematic for Catholic educators and especially for theologians. Part of the anomaly is that the requirement of the *mandatum* affects only those Catholic theologians teaching in Catholic universities; it does not affect those teaching in other institutions. The *mandatum* is defined as an acknowledgment that the professor teaches within the full communion of the Catholic Church. But once granted by authority, a *mandatum* can also be withdrawn. Many Catholic educators and theologians worry that this could jeopardize both the academic freedom of the theologian and the institutional autonomy of the university. Thus most administrators and theologians have been reluctant to embrace the requirement of the *mandatum*.

But if Catholic universities are to successfully make the case that their religious identity can be protected and served apart from Vatican mandated juridical norms, then it is incumbent on them to take concrete steps to do so. As Steinfels has observed, "nurturing a Catholic identity demands a whole repertoire of initiatives that stretch from student life to recruitment of key faculty and administrators, from campus ministry to new course development, from research incentives to interdisciplinary conversations."[11]

Theology and Religious Studies

Nurturing a university's Catholic identity is not the sole responsibility of the theology or religious studies department. As Steinfels has argued,

---

[10] "An Application to the United States of *Ex Corde Ecclesiae*" *Origins* 29/16 (1999) 245–54; the amended and approved version appears in *Origins* 29/25 (1999) 401–09.

[11] Steinfels, "A Journalist's View: Does Rome Have the Best Answer?" *Commonweal* 126/7 (1999) 15.

It is a tragedy that efforts to implement *Ex Corde Ecclesiae* have so misdirected energy and attention to the certification and standing of theology professors. With most Catholic schools requiring no more than two semesters of theology, those courses could meet the severest standards of orthodoxy without guaranteeing any significant grappling with the Catholic heritage if it is not present elsewhere in the curriculum.[12]

The way that theology is practiced and taught in Catholic colleges and universities has changed considerably in the years since the Second Vatican Council. Today it is not at all uncommon for a Catholic student to take for his or her requirement in this area a course in world religion and another on marriage, Judaism, or perhaps one in religion and film, often explaining that they have already "had enough theology."

Theology is always a critical reflection on the faith of the Christian community, done by members of that community. Prior to the council, the study of theology took place largely in seminaries; it was a clerical endeavor, taught by priests for seminarians. Students in Catholic colleges and universities, including Jesuit ones, didn't study theology; they took courses in "religion." The courses were largely apologetic in nature, concerned with doctrinal orthodoxy and religious formation. They met fewer hours per week, received less academic credit, and were generally taught by priest instructors who lacked the academic credentials increasingly expected in other departments.[13]

For example at my own institution, the name of the Department of Religion was changed to Theology only in 1962. Until then courses met two hours per week for one unit of credit (rather than the usual three). It was only in 1972 that a major was introduced and the department was renamed Religious Studies. In 1980 the name was changed to Theology and later to Theological Studies. The discipline of theology itself changed considerably in the period after the council. The first doctoral program in theology open to laymen and women (called "religious studies" to head off possible objections from Rome) was established at Marquette University in 1963.[14] Other Catholic universities quickly followed Marquette's lead. As laymen and increasingly laywomen completed their

---

[12] Steinfels, "Catholic Identity," 175.

[13] See Robert J. Wister, "The Teaching of Theology 1950–1990: The American Catholic Experience," *America* 162 (1990) 92.

[14] In Germany the Ludwig Maximilian Universität in Munich began admitting laymen into their graduate program in theology in 1951.

degrees through these programs and began moving into faculty positions in Catholic colleges and universities, the locus of theological scholarship began to shift, from seminaries to universities and graduate schools. For example, *Theological Studies*, the premiere Catholic theological journal in the U.S., was originally a journal largely for seminary professors. In its first decade (1940–49), 144 out of 185 articles were written by seminary professors. In its fifth decade (1980–89), only 63 articles came from those involved in seminaries; 199 were from professors in colleges or universities.[15]

The laicization and professionalization that Catholic theology has undergone in the years since the council mean that the majority of Catholic theologians today are laypeople, much less subject to ecclesiastical authority than their clerical and religious predecessors. Moreover many of those hired are non-Catholics who did their graduate work in non-Catholic institutions or Catholics from these same schools, thus educated outside their own tradition. Their professional standards are determined, not by the Church, but by the academy, by their various professional associations. The requirement that Catholic theologians seek a *mandatum* represents an attempt to curb their independence, particularly what is seen by Church authorities as their "dissent" on controversial issues. But this risks damaging the hard won reputation for freedom of inquiry and scholarship that Catholic departments of theology and religious studies have achieved.

However Catholic theologians also need to recognize that among the publics they address is the Church, which implies some accountability. When a position taken by a theologian is contrary to official Catholic teaching, the bishop has every right to say so publicly. But adding a further juridical relationship is more problematic, as it could suggest episcopal interference in academic affairs. Ecclesial communion is far better served by relationships of mutual respect and collaboration.

At my university the members of the Department of Theological Studies are strongly committed to the university's Catholic identity. They serve on Archdiocesan commissions such as its Theological Commission, are members of various ecumenical and interreligious dialogues, assist in the preparation of pastoral letters and statements, help to design formation programs for lay pastoral associates, and are frequent presenters at Archdiocesan congresses and assemblies. The non-Catholic members

---

[15] Michael A. Fahey, "Farewell from the Editor's Desk," *Theological Studies* 66/4 (2005) 737.

of the department are also involved in these works on behalf of the Church. They are respected and valued for their contribution and are not second-class citizens. Many Catholic university faculties of theology enjoy similar cordial relationships with their bishops.

I do not mean to suggest that Catholic theology departments are always beyond criticism. By no means! Those who teach theology in Catholic universities should be concerned with handing on the Catholic tradition in its fullness and not just the latest theories of the academy. Their theology should be rooted in the life and faith of the Church; that is to say, it should be ecclesial. As Haughey says, theology "is a discipline only because there has been and still are churches that mediate and celebrate faith in Christ. Faith remains the formal object of theology. No faith, no theology. No church, no faith, at least of a Christian character."[16]

The late Monika Hellwig, an outstanding theologian who spent the last years of her life as executive director of the Association of Catholic Colleges and Universities, lays at least part of the responsibility for the lack of familiarity of Catholic university students with their own tradition at the doors of their theology and religious studies departments. She notes that parents and others outside the universities expect that their theology departments will hand on an understanding of their Catholic faith tradition, doing in effect an advanced catechesis or what used to be called positive theology. However most faculty members in those departments take the position that the time for catechesis is long past. They are more concerned with exploring new territory, assessing experience, and helping the students to form their own critical judgments. And of course, pursuing their own research. Their theology programs are designed to introduce students to unfamiliar traditions and are often taught from a non-confessional, "ecumenical" perspective. But such an undifferentiated approach does not represent true ecumenism.

Hellwig suggests that we need to consider "whether our student bodies are sufficiently grounded in their own tradition to be genuinely ecumenical in their study rather than simply confused."[17] She asks "whether we should be offering, at least to those undergraduate students who choose it, a sequence of courses giving them cumulatively a thorough understanding of Catholic tradition at an intellectually advanced level."[18]

---

[16] Haughey, "Theology and the Mission," 13.

[17] Monika Hellwig, "Theology at Catholic Universities: The Situation and its Possibilities," *Origins* 32/43 (2003) 708.

[18] Ibid., 709.

But this is not always done in Catholic universities. I remember checking the theology offerings several years ago while on sabbatical at one of our more prestigious Jesuit universities. Among the plethora of courses on world religions, Asian, Buddhist, Hindu, Jewish, or Islamic religion, feminist and womanist theology, race, gender, and religion, the Church and homosexuality, ritual, comparative mythologies, and psychology and religion was one course on Catholicism and one on the New Testament. There was a God course but nothing on Christology, Church, or sacrament.

My department is strongly committed to the religious mission of our university and its members to the life of the Church. Yet in an age when many have called attention to the religious and theological illiteracy of so many young Catholics, a recent comment of our students is very telling. When surveyed by a faculty committee reviewing the theology major, they collectively responded that "they had been better instructed in modern and postmodern developments and critiques of the tradition than in the tradition itself." The students see the problem, even if their professors do not.

While departments of theology or religious studies in Catholic higher educational institutions can play an important role in serving the religious identity of these institutions, they cannot be expected to bear this responsibility alone. If Catholic universities are to successfully make the case that their religious identity can be protected and served apart from Vatican mandated juridical norms, then it is incumbent on them to take concrete steps to do so.

Preserving Catholic Identity

How can Catholic colleges or universities safeguard and enhance their religious mission and identity without loosing their integrity as institutions of higher education? Too often the importance of Catholic identity is affirmed, while no real steps are taken to preserve or enhance it. Responsibility for mission and identity cannot be left to the department of theology or religious studies or to campus ministry. It involves the entire university community, faculty, staff, and administration.

Nor can Catholic colleges and universities be held hostage to pressure groups like the Cardinal Newman Society, a self-appointed group of conservative Catholics established in 1993. The group monitors Catholic institutions in the name of strengthening their Catholic identity, but their approach is mainly negative. Issues prominent on their website include insisting that theology teachers on Catholic campuses are certified by their bishops as teaching in accord with Catholic doctrine, preventing the performance of Eve Ensler's controversial feminist play "The Vagina Monologues," protesting appearances by political figures who have supported pro-abortion legislation, and identifying "dissidents and heretics on Catholic theological faculties." The institutions envisioned by the Cardinal Newman Society would be strongly committed to a single "orthodox" view, but they would not be genuine universities, committed to the search for truth in the context of a full exchange of ideas.

In January 2006, Archbishop John Vlazny, retiring chair of the Bishops and Presidents Committee, established by the United States Council of Catholic Bishops, wrote to those U.S. bishops listed as the Cardinal Newman Society's ecclesiastical advisors. Noting that the committee's members had been monitoring the Cardinal Newman's Society's publications and positions, he said that they had "found them often aggressive, inaccurate, or lacking in balance," misrepresenting the Catholic colleges and universities they criticized.[19]

In the remainder of this chapter I would like to consider a number of key areas that need to be addressed, if a Catholic identity is to be preserved without loss to the academic integrity of these institutions. They include hiring, curriculum, Catholic Studies programs, and residence life.

Hiring for Mission

Many Catholic colleges and universities today approach the hiring of faculty from the perspective of "hiring for mission." But if the concept is critical, it is also controversial. Even raising the issue makes some faculty members and administrators nervous. They worry about "confessional" requirements, or about making non-Catholic faculty and staff feel less welcome. Safeguarding a university's Catholic identity does not mean that everyone has to be Catholic. But potential faculty must buy into the university's mission and institutional identity.

John Langan insists that for maintaining the Catholic identity of a university the crucial criterion is intellectual interest and competence in

---

[19] Cited in "Measuring Catholic Identity," *America* 194/11 (March 27, 2006) Editorial.

matters that form part of the Catholic tradition.[20] Non-Catholic faculty members should never be treated unfairly or made to feel as though they are second-class citizens. That includes those for whom developing Catholic intellectual and academic life is not a priority; they are often significant contributors to the growth and well-being of the university.[21]

Without giving up a commitment to diversity, new faculty members need to be introduced to the mission and identity of the university at the time of their hiring. They should be asked specifically in the hiring process how they might support and contribute to these values, not simply whether they are "comfortable" with the university's religious mission. In some departments faculty members are unwilling to do this, and so it plays no part in their hiring practice. While most Catholic universities subscribe to the "critical mass" theory of Catholic faculty presence, most do not keep statistics showing how many Catholics are actually on their faculties. Richard H. Passon observes that no Jesuit university in the U.S. has formally implemented a "critical mass" policy, though Notre Dame has utilized it in a recent institutional plan.[22] Steinfels mentions that the Notre Dame faculty is 55 percent Catholic, while at Georgetown, which does not keep a record, he says he "often met faculty members . . . who told me that they had come to the university with little awareness that it was Catholic or Jesuit."[23]

Some institutions speak generally about hiring for mission, though without clear strategies for doing so. Such language can easily become nothing more than "boiler plate." Catholic universities need men and women who can be bearers of the tradition, a role that cannot be left to the diminishing number of religious on campus.

Steinfels argues that "the place in hiring of religious commitment and religious interests and competencies in research and teaching must be confronted, and clear, meaningful policies developed."[24] He quotes Marsden's words: "Once a church-related institution adopts the policy that it will hire simply 'the best qualified candidates,' it is simply a matter of time until its faculty will have an ideological profile essentially like that of the faculty at every other mainstream university."[25] Thus it might

---

[20] John Langan, "Reforging Catholic Identity," 22.

[21] Ibid., 23.

[22] Richard H. Passon, "Hiring for Mission: An Overview," *Conversations* 12 (Fall 1997) 9; this issue of *Conversations* is entirely devoted to hiring for mission.

[23] Steinfels, *A People Adrift* (New York: Simon and Schuster, 2003) 140.

[24] Steinfels, "Catholic Identity," 176.

[25] Ibid., 175.

be good to adopt what Paul Wilkes calls "a preferential option for faith."[26] Without a strong presence of committed Catholics on a university faculty, it is difficult to see how an institution can have a Catholic identity.

Curriculum

Another key area is the curriculum. Does the curriculum foster a Christian humanism, centered on the dignity of the human person and the importance of community? Does it communicate a strong sense for the values and culture of the Catholic tradition? Does it teach students to think theologically? Do they learn the Catholic stories? Can they read religious texts in a way that is at once critical and at the same time honors them? Do they see the connection between their faith and life in the world? Again to quote Steinfels:

> Today's consensus has gone beyond polemical questions like, Is there a Catholic mathematics, a Catholic chemistry, a Catholic accounting or a Catholic business administration? It recognizes that the rich Catholic intellectual heritage which should be communicated, explored, questioned, revised and renewed does not pertain in precisely the same way and to the same extent to every field and discipline. But while that heritage could be less obviously relevant to chemistry and accounting than to political theory or literature, even chemistry and mathematics departments, let alone business administration, might be hospitable to certain philosophical, ethics or cross-disciplinary reflections and conversations that are unlikely to occur elsewhere.[27]

It has often been said that a Catholic university is where the Church does its thinking. In Jesuit universities, the mission of the university is said to include the service of the faith and the promotion of justice, language taken from the Thirty-Second General Congregation of the Society of Jesus (1974–75). Many of these institutions have written this language into their mission statements.

Jesuits have held up the example of the Universidad Centroamericana in El Salvador (UCA), where six Jesuit teachers and administrators, as

---

[26] Paul Wilkes, "Catholic Spoken Here: A Report from the Academic Front," *America* 180/15 (1999) 18.

[27] Steinfels, "Catholic Identity," 175.

well as their cook and her daughter, were murdered by Salvadoran military forces in 1989. Though by no means a university *of* the poor, the university had clearly made an option *for* the poor. Under the leadership of Ignatio Ellacuría, the rector-president, and Ignacio Martín-Baró, a University of Chicago-trained social psychologist, the UCA had sought to cast light on the reality of Salvadoran life (*la realidad nacional*) through its teaching, research, and what it called *proyección social*, that is, all the ways the university projects the results of its research, analysis, and proposed solutions into the society of which it is a part.[28]

Jon Sobrino, a theologian on the UCA faculty, absent the night his fellow Jesuits were killed, has argued that a Catholic university cannot remain disengaged from a world in which there is so much suffering and injustice. Compassion for the disadvantaged must be its central concern. Stephen Pope has contrasted Sobrino's views with those of John Henry Newman who argued in his *The Idea of a University* that a university is a place where knowledge is pursued for its own sake. Pope takes the position that both views have something to say to a Catholic university; intellectual development is always key, but in a Catholic university it always needs to be cultivated in a context that includes the Catholic and Christian values of love of God and love of neighbor.[29]

If the language of "faith and justice" seeks to focus mission and identity, it can easily become no more than rhetoric. What university does not claim a concern for social justice? And many today offer the study of religion. At its best, Catholic higher education seeks to integrate faith and reason in a way that allows God's self-revelation in Christ and the Gospel Jesus proclaimed to illumine and take root in culture. This is what both Pope Paul VI and Pope John Paul II call the evangelization of culture.

But I wonder to what extent the Catholic intellectual tradition really informs our curriculums? Most university bulletins list special studies programs in the following areas: African-American, Alcohol and Drug, Asian/Pacific, Chicana/Chicano, Gay and Lesbian, Irish, as well as Liberal, Peace, Urban, and Women's Studies. Shouldn't Catholic Studies be among them? Today some secular universities are adding chairs or programs in Catholic studies. If a secular university like Stanford can

[28] See Dean Brackley, "Higher Standards for Higher Education: The Christian University and Solidarity," *Listening: A Journal of Religion and Culture* (2002) 20.

[29] Stephen Pope, "A Vocation for Catholic Higher Education," *Commonweal* 124/6 (March 28, 1997) 13.

offer a course on "American Catholic Writers,"[30] one might hope to find such courses at a Catholic university. And even more, a Catholic Studies program.

Catholic Studies Programs

In the mid-1990s Catholic colleges and universities began inaugurating Catholic Studies programs to introduce the richness of the Catholic tradition to their students.[31] Francesco Cesareo points out that curricular changes in the latter half of the twentieth century led to a scarcity of courses rooted in the Catholic intellectual tradition, resulting in "graduates from Catholic colleges and universities with little or no understanding of Catholicism. Unfamiliar with the great thinkers and classics of the Catholic intellectual tradition, the very future of that tradition was at stake."[32]

De Paul University in Chicago, Marquette, St. Louis, and John Carroll began Catholic Studies programs in 1997. The Institute for Catholic Studies at John Carroll includes an undergraduate minor, faculty development forums, a public lecture series, and a magazine. The minor concludes with a capstone course called "Great Thinkers of the Catholic Intellectual Tradition." The program also offers a ten-day Spring Break course in Rome on the church in Rome that includes meetings with various Vatican officials; a semester in Rome at the Pontifical University of St. Thomas (the Angelicum) is also possible. At the University of Dayton, Catholic Studies is integrated into the core curriculum so that a student may choose a course in the Catholic intellectual tradition from among seven interdisciplinary themes such as ecology, globalism, or social justice, designed to integrate the general education requirements.

Fordham University launched its University Center for American Catholic Studies in 2001, an interdisciplinary program modeled on Notre Dame's Cushwa Center for the Study of American Catholicism. It sponsors public lectures, seminars led by faculty members diverse in their

---

[30] Cf. Albert Gelpi, "The Catholic Presence in American Culture," *American Literary History* 11/1 (1999) 201.

[31] See Thomas M. Landy, "Catholic Studies at Catholic Colleges and Universities," in *Enhancing Religious Identity: Best Practices from Catholic Campuses*, ed. John Wilcox and Irene King (Washington, D.C.: Georgetown University Press, 2000) 218–25.

[32] Francesco C. Cesareo, "Catholic Studies and the Recovery of the Catholic Intellectual Tradition," *Connections: Association of Jesuit Colleges and Universities* (March 2003) 10.

cultural or religious backgrounds that examine issues such as religion and violence, Catholicism and public education, and anti-Catholicism. A recent conference examined the work of Joseph Fitzpatrick, S.J., known for his work with immigrants. Jeffrey von Arx, S.J., then Dean of Fordham College, said that the Center would provide a "focus where this University's distinctive mission of serious intellectual engagement with the religious identity that is at its heart can take place."[33]

In 2002 St. Louis renamed its program the Manresa Program in Catholic/Jesuit Studies, built around a six-course sequence. It has a foundations course, four cross-listed electives, and a capstone course. It also includes a monthly movie night on classic films like *The Mission* or *A Man For All Seasons* and field trips to nearby religious sites, for instance, a monastery. Perhaps the most successful program is at the University of St. Thomas in Minnesota. Its Department of Catholic Studies offers an undergraduate minor and major as well as an M.A. degree and a joint J.D.-M.A. in Catholic Studies. It also includes the opportunity of doing a semester or a year at the Angelicum in Rome, a Catholic studies club, and a Catholic studies floor in a residence hall.

Key to all these programs is a multidisciplinary approach. Rather than focusing simply on theology and philosophy, they involve courses as well in literature, art, history, political science, film, and communications so that students can come to appreciate Catholicism as a culture, a worldview, and a way of life. But some faculty members resist such programs, fearing that they will serve some conservative or "restorationist" agenda. Others fear that a Catholic Studies program might exclude non-Catholic faculty members. But there is no reason why non-Catholic professors could not offer Catholic Studies courses in areas of their expertise, for example, on religious themes in medieval art or in the thought of Thomas Aquinas. Some institutions offer faculty grants to develop such courses.

Andrew Greeley has asked why Catholic undergraduate schedules of courses list so few courses that might provide the nucleus for a Catholic studies program:

> Why not offer courses in poetry, fiction, literature, art, music, social theory, history? The history of the papacy? . . . Catholic novels of initiation? Catholic perspectives on fantasy and on science fiction

---

[33] James T. Fisher, "The Center for American Catholic Studies," *Connections: Association of Jesuit Colleges and Universities* (March 2003) 9.

and film? God in the movies? The nude in Catholic art? Varieties of Catholic spirituality? Crucial Catholic thinkers? Mary in the Catholic heritage? Major traditions in Catholic mysticism? Contemporary Catholic theologians? Images of Jesus in art and literature?[34]

There are other programs and initiatives that can support Catholic identity. One expects to find a chapel prominently located on a Catholic university campus, religious iconography in halls and buildings symbolizing its faith, and specific commitments articulated in its mission statement. Service learning programs involve students in real-life problems off campus and "alternative Spring Breaks" offer opportunities to travel and develop a sense of solidarity with the disadvantaged in countries like Guatemala and El Salvador, or closer to home, in Appalachia. Some institutions are establishing centers for the spiritual development of faculty members and staff; Boston College, Creighton University, Marquette, and Loyola Marymount each have a Center for Ignatius Spirituality. Seattle University and John Carroll have similar centers. Others have seminars on the institution's religious mission for faculty and staff. Most of the 28 Jesuit universities in the U.S. have administrators for mission and identity, ten of them with vice-presidential status so that they can participate in the top level of university governance.[35]

Occasionally efforts to symbolize an institution's Catholic identity are complicated by the cultural wars endemic to the academy or diluted by attempts to be "inclusive." One major Jesuit university was caught up in a six-month debate over whether or not crucifixes in its classrooms would be offensive to those of other faith traditions, finally deciding to display them, "as long as they are artistic." Another has no campus chapel, aside from a parish church, and no daily liturgies for the students. One beautiful chapel on campus was turned into offices. Its university ministry sponsors retreats that are not specifically Christian, let alone Catholic, except for one silent Ignatian retreat. It hosts a conservative evangelical fellowship, but no similar group for Catholics, with the result that some Catholic students looking for a more intense spiritual life join the evangelicals. At other Jesuit institutions, administrators sometimes give in to marketing analysts who argue "Jesuit sells, Catholic does not."

[34] Greeley, "A Sociologist's View: What Catholics Do Well," *Commonweal* 126 (1999) 20–21.

[35] The latter include Boston College, Fordham, Georgetown, Gonzaga, Loyola of Chicago, Regis, St. Joseph's, Scranton, Seattle, and Xavier.

Residence Life

A final area that is of concern to many faculty members and administrators today is that of residence life. This is a sensitive issue. Most Catholic colleges and universities have a large proportion of resident students who live in campus halls and apartments, under the supervision of student "resident advisors." Since these schools no longer attempt to function *in loco parentis*, it is difficult to say how the culture of our resident life communities differ from what one would find at any secular university. In the words of a student activities administrator, there is too much "sex, drugs, and rock and roll." If drug use is generally down today, alcohol abuse remains a problem. Binge drinking and "partying" at night makes it difficult for many students to study and results in poor class attendance. Some come to class under the influence. On many campuses there are no restrictions on men or women visiting each other's residences at any hour of the day or night. While housing contracts generally proscribe overnight guests of the opposite sex, many of the students are sexually active and those cohabiting are rarely disciplined. Nor are resident advisors adequately trained to project values in this area.

I once heard a resident advisor explain to her incoming residents that overnight visitors of the opposite sex were not allowed "because this is a Jesuit/Marymount university." At Georgetown University some years ago, the Student Life division sponsored a program to instruct the students in the use of contraceptives. Health Service staffers occasionally embarrass administrators when they list in their student materials abortion agencies, which then later turn up on the university's webpage. At Loyola Marymount, the resident advisors were provided copies of a book entitled *Sexual Etiquette 101*, a graphic approach to sex complete with "how-to" pictures which took a permissive approach to sexual conduct. For example, it counseled that some people prefer sex without intercourse, others mutual masturbation, some intercourse, and some prefer abstinence.[36] One suggestion to new couples was that they might purchase condoms on the first date. The highest norm seems to be, "keep it safe, and keep it consensual." Of course most student life administrators were embarrassed when controversy broke out over the book, but we need to ask, what sort of message are we communicating to our students?

---

[36] Robert A. Hatcher, et al., *Sexual Etiquette 101 & More* (Dawsonville, GA: Bridging the Gap Communications, 2001).

In a recent article, Vigen Guroian, a professor of moral theology at Loyola College of Baltimore, describes a campus culture of binge drinking, "hook ups," sex in a roommate's presence, and a peer pressure that makes promiscuity practically obligatory. He concludes that his institution

> and a great many other colleges and universities simply do not acknowledge, let alone address, the sexualization of the American college. Rather, they do everything possible to put a smiley face on an unhealthy and morally destructive environment, one that—and this is no small matter—also makes serious academic study next to impossible. Most of the rhetoric one hears incessantly from American colleges about caring for young men and women and respecting their freedom and maturity is disingenuous.[37]

Some students have little sense for the common good of the resident community. Trashing of dorms occurs too often. Those apprehended for triggering false fire alarms or doing willful damage to their residence halls will get other students to testify in hearings before juridical officers that they were elsewhere at the time.

Although many of our resident students are generous in service and a good number are involved in Christian Life Communities, it is difficult to see that there is anything specifically Christian or Catholic about the culture of our residence life communities. Concerns for privacy, student rights, diversity, and competition with other schools makes it difficult to address these issues. Father William Watson in a article in *America* magazine raised the sensitive question of how our schools can shape what he calls "the ethics of personal conduct" when so many of those in our student life departments come out of secular university backgrounds. They are often unfamiliar, he argues, with what the Catholic tradition has to say about spirituality, sexual morality, and interpersonal relationships.[38] But it is these "professionals" who shape the culture of our residence communities.

---

[37] Vigen Guroian, "The New Debauchery and the Colleges that Let It Happen," *Christianity Today* 49/2 (February 2005) 50–51; the sexualization of American youth is not limited to college students; see Caitlin Flanagan, "Are You There God? It's Me, Monica. How Nice Girls Get so Casual about Oral Sex," *The Atlantic* 297/1 (January–February, 2006) 167–82.

[38] William M. Watson, "Pastoral Reflections on Catholic Higher Education," *America* 180/18 (1999) 8.

There are some initiatives to address the special needs of resident students. Santa Clara University plans to move all its resident students into "learning communities" where residents live together in communities, often with faculty members among them, for four years. In the first couple of years after this program began, the annual cost for end-of-the-year damage to the residence halls decreased dramatically.

Conclusion

In an address at the University of Notre Dame, Archbishop J. Michael Miller, Secretary of the Vatican Congregation for Catholic Education, raised the question as to whether or not Pope Benedict XVI might follow a policy of "evangelical pruning," that is, no longer claiming as Catholic those institutions that are no longer motivated by a strong sense of Catholic identity.[39] This represents a radical approach, but is also evidence of concern in high places.

A Catholic university has many elements which embody its religious identity. They include an institutional commitment to the Catholic tradition, departments of philosophy and theology, the values and religious commitment of its faculty, campus ministry, the ethos of the campus, and an ability to celebrate its life in iconography, ritual, and liturgy. But a university cannot maintain this Catholic identity without a firm commitment on the part of all in the university community, particularly faculty and administrators. Nor can Catholic identity be reduced to a concern for social justice or diversity; neither trumps the university's religious mission.

Those parents who are sending their children to Catholic schools—at great expense—are rightfully concerned about the Catholic identity of those institutions. They see their investment as part of their own responsibility to pass on the faith to their children and make the sacrifice willingly. We have considered in this chapter some of the efforts made by those institutions to safeguard and enhance their Catholic identity.

However only a small percentage of Catholic students (524,658) attend a Catholic college or university. The 2005 *NCR* survey of American Catholics reported that only 12 percent of post–Vatican II Catholics attended a Catholic college or university, and only 29 percent attended a Catholic

---

[39] J. Michael Miller, "Catholic Universities and Their Catholic Identity," *Origins* 35/27 (2005) 454–55.

high school.[40] The great majority of Catholic university students attend public or private, non-Catholic schools, where it is estimated that Catholic enrollment is between 30 to 40 percent.[41] This means that the vast majority of young Catholics have never taken a university-level course in theology.

For most young Catholics, their religious education ends with completing the eighth grade or with confirmation. No wonder so many know so little about their faith. Not a few of them, when confronted with a problem or challenge, end up leaving the Church. While some non-Catholic institutions are establishing chairs in Catholic studies, the Church often lacks the resources to support effective ministries in these schools.

---

[40] See "Survey of U.S. Catholics," *National Catholic Reporter*, 41/42 (September 30, 2005) 9–24, Table 14.

[41] James Davidson, "Where Do Catholic Students Go To College," *The Tidings* (August 15, 2003) 12.

Chapter 6

A New Generation?

What about the next generation of Catholics? Is there any evidence that younger Catholics are moving in a more traditional direction? Davidson and Hoge argue that they have not found evidence of this in their surveys. In *Young Adult Catholics* Hoge estimated that the sample studied contained perhaps ten percent identified as "core Catholics," regular in their practice, unwilling to separate spirituality from Church, taking papal teaching seriously (even when disagreeing with particulars), and enriching their spiritual life with sacraments, Marian devotion, and to a lesser degree, devotion to the saints.[1] In the Notre Dame study, Hoge and Davidson report that the millennial generation, the youngest, is not markedly different from the post–Vatican II generation.[2]

But a number of commentators such as Katarina Schuth, Robert Schreiter, and William Portier have noted a different attitude among many young Catholics today, particularly those who are preparing for leadership roles in the Church or taking on a more active role in its life. These include not just seminarians, religious, and younger members of the theological academy, but also other young adults, some of them still undergraduate students. Something indeed seems to be changing in the Catholic community. A new generation of adult Catholics is emerging, some of whom seem to be more passionate about their faith, more ecclesial in its expression, and more concerned with their identity precisely as Catholic Christians.

---

[1] Dean R. Hoge, William D. Dinges, Mary Johnson, Juan L. Gonzales, Jr., *Young Adult Catholics: Religion in the Culture of Choice* (Notre Dame, IN: University of Notre Dame Press, 2001) 172.

[2] James D. Davidson and Dean R. Hoge, "Catholics After the Scandal: A New Study's New Findings," *Commonweal* 131/20 (November 19, 2004) 19.

While some commentators are not sure how to describe this group, others over fifty voice concern about a new conservatism.

Although Colleen Carroll's *The New Faithful* overstates the case, her book is one indication that something new is happening. She argues that a growing number of young Americans, both Catholic and Protestant, are forsaking the liberalism and religious relativism of their parents' generation and turning to a more traditional Christianity that she calls simply "orthodoxy."[3] She sees the Catholics among them as welcoming guidance from traditional sources of authority, including Pope John Paul II. Many admired him for his uncompromising teaching. Some are converts, or have had the experience of rediscovering their faith as young adults, or are "reverts" returning to Catholicism as "evangelical Catholics" after becoming involved in other churches. With one out of four of them children of divorced parents, Carroll suggests that they are part of a new sexual revolution that prizes chastity, rejects sex before marriage and abortion, and opposes homosexual activity, though they insist that homosexuals have the right to be treated as equals.

Carroll is obviously focusing on a small subgroup. Her book suffers from a too narrow construal of orthodoxy, identifying it with an equally narrow traditionalism and with religious communities and movements like the Legionaries of Christ, Regnum Christi, and Opus Dei. But she is not alone in seeing something new and different. Other commentators have noticed something distinctive about younger Catholics today.

David Whalen, a professor at St. Michael's College, Toronto, did his doctoral work on ministerial identity. He also has called attention to the emergence of a distinctive but growing group he has met in his classes and his community's formation program. He calls them "contemporary traditionalists." While they seem supportive of Church teaching on divorce, remarriage, and homosexuality, he describes them as often appealing to a "notwithstanding" clause which admits of exceptions. Though they are strongly against abortion, they are not terribly concerned about contraception. Rather than seeing their approach as representing a "cafeteria theology" or situational ethics, these young adults see it as an *interim* theology. More comfortable with traditional piety, eucharistic adoration, and Taizé prayer they seem less interested in informal liturgies and shared homilies. They have no problem expressing their religious beliefs, but even those studying theology seem to be quite lacking in even a basic

---

[3] Colleen Carroll, *The New Faithful: Why Young Adults Are Embracing Christian Orthodoxy* (Chicago: Loyola Press, 2002).

theological literacy. He says that they are much more likely to have on their shelves a copy of the new *Catechism of the Catholic Church* than the documents of Vatican II. Whalen identifies these contemporary traditionalists as the ones most likely to pursue consecrated life or the priesthood today.[4]

A new outreach, the Fellowship of Catholic University Students (FOCUS), offers another example. Founded in 1998, FOCUS now has some one hundred staff members and two thousand students active on twenty-seven campuses, both secular and Catholic, in fifteen states. Citing Pope John Paul II's challenge, "I ask you young people . . . to be prophets of life," their mission statement says the following: "When college students make the heroic decision to give their lives to Jesus Christ, they gain true Vision of Life: for leadership in college, and for making an impact after graduation. FOCUS helps college students to allow Jesus Christ to be the Lord of their lives—including their studies, social life, dating relationships, and major life decisions."[5]

If there is a new generation of Catholics emerging with different concerns, they are not all identified with the most conservative expressions of contemporary Catholicism. In this chapter we will consider some representatives of this new generation. They include those some describe as "evangelical Catholics," John Paul II Catholics, seminarians, young theologians, various converts, and "reverts."

Evangelical Catholics

William Portier refers to this new group of young adults as "evangelical Catholics," with a nod to David O'Brien and Keith Fournier who have also used the term. He observes that by the 1990s a new breed of students started turning up in his theology classes. "Far from a majority, their small number often includes the most intellectually gifted. These students are interested in Catholic-specific issues. They want meat. They love the pope. They are pro-life. They do service trips during breaks and gravitate toward 'service' upon graduation." They do not fit easily into the liberal/conservative categories of the fifty-plus generation and most

---

[4] David M. Whalen, "The Emergence of the Contemporary Traditionalists," *Review for Religious* 61 (November–December 2002) 585–93.

[5] www.focusonline.org.

of them refuse to separate "orthodoxy" from social justice.[6] Unlike John Haughey's experience of Catholic students reluctant to share their faith, these students combine traditional Catholic practices with public witness and evangelizing strategies from Campus Crusade or InterVarsity Fellowship.[7]

But Portier uses "evangelical" in a distinctive sense. Usually the term refers to born again Bible Christians. Portier's primary reference is neither charismatic Catholics nor converts from evangelicalism, though he does not exclude them, but rather those who come to the evangelical-Catholic confluence from the Catholic side of the spectrum. They resemble evangelicals in the sociological sense of the "voluntary" character of their commitment, with a religious identity that is chosen rather than inherited or ethnic.[8] Like those described by Hoge in *Young Adult Catholics*, they come out of a culture of religious pluralism and are choosing their own form of Christianity. Because they stand out from other Catholics because of their "strong and vital religious tradition," Portier sees them as most resembling evangelical Protestants.[9]

Portier thinks that this group should not be ignored. Noting that most commentators focus on the majority of loosely affiliated young adult Catholics, he turns instead to the not insignificant minority, the 37 percent that score high on Davidson's index of traditional beliefs and practices, including the 30 percent that think that the Catholic Church is the one true church, the 20 percent who think that premarital sex is always wrong, and the 14 percent that disagree that one can be a good Catholic without going to Mass. He asks, Are they "leftovers or prophets?" While Davidson queries the data in terms of a return to the past, Portier asks instead if post–subculture conditions are giving rise to new kinds of Catholics. "Do they represent the past, as Davidson's language suggests, or do they represent the future?"[10]

I've seen signs of a change much like Portier is describing among some of the students I teach. One recent freshman was wearing a "Cardinal Joseph Ratzinger Fan Club" T-shirt, with the cardinal's statement that

[6] William L. Portier, "Here Come the Evangelical Catholics," *Communio* 31 (Spring 2004) 37.

[7] Ibid., 55; see John C. Haughey, "Why Are Catholics Slow to Profess Their Faith? Church-ianity and Christ-ianity," *America* 190/18 (2004) 8–9.

[8] Portier, "Here Come the Evangelical Catholics," 39–40.

[9] Ibid., 51.

[10] Portier, "Here Come the Evangelical Catholics," 52; Davidson, *The Search for Common Ground: What Unites and Divides Catholic Americans* (Huntington, IN: Our Sunday Visitor Publishing, 1997) 133.

"truth is not determined by a majority vote" printed on the back. A convert to Catholicism in high school, he had attended the 2005 World Youth Day in Cologne. Sitting beside him in class were two friends, both enthusiastic fans of Karl Keating and *Catholic Answers*. Others are more comfortable with external signs of devotion, kneeling on the floor in the front row of the chapel after communion, bowing reverently before receiving the host, or wearing T-shirts proclaiming "Ten Reasons I'm Proud that I'm Catholic." They are strongly pro-life and support eucharistic adoration. They do not usually buy into the reformist agenda espoused by the Vatican II generation. Few of the women in this group are concerned about inclusive language and they are not uniformly in favor of the ordination of women. While they take for granted equality of opportunity and remuneration, few would identify themselves as feminists. What was especially impressive to me about these students was not just their enthusiasm for Catholicism; they also knew their Scriptures, could tell the stories, identify the characters, interpret the texts. This alone made them stand out from most of the other students in the class, whose knowledge of the Bible was next to nil.

Portier faults both Davidson and Hoge for not looking more carefully at the obvious religious vitality represented by these evangelical Catholics, attributing their lack of interest to an inordinate fear of sectarianism.[11] "Aging theologians are generally blind to the significance of these people because in 1968 terms, their behavior is 'conservative.' But evangelical Catholics have never been to where their elders think they want to return."[12]

Seminarians

Seminarians and young religious represent another example of changing attitudes among young Catholics. Many commentators have complained about the conservative attitudes of many in seminaries and religious formation programs today. Katarina Schuth has done considerable research on these groups. Seminary faculty members she surveyed report an increasing tendency toward external practices of piety more characteristic of the 1950s, more conservative liturgical attitudes, and more interest in habits, vestments, and Church paraphernalia, traditional music, and devotions, "an increasingly reactionary stance toward

[11] Portier, "Here Come the Evangelical Catholics," 53–54.
[12] Ibid., 55.

moderate views on authority and liturgical law," and a need to hold in check faculty and students with regard to ritual, dogma, and ecclesiastical prescriptions.[13]

In a more recent study, she identifies diversity as the most obvious characteristic of those preparing for ministry in seminaries and theologates. Many seminarians today come from Latin America, Europe, Asia, or Africa and are generally older than the seminarians of an earlier generation. Many theologates include sizable numbers of lay men and women as well as candidates for the priesthood.[14] Both groups, whether clerical or lay, include many who lack familiarity with the Catholic tradition. They "are relatively uninformed about Church teachings" and "lack a vocabulary to help them form a Catholic identity and interpret their Catholic experiences."[15] Most came of age after Vatican II and have no memory of the Church before 1970.

Schuth breaks this population down into four groups. The first is comprised of the minority who are deeply rooted in their faith and highly motivated, generally coming from families who practiced their faith. They are more familiar with the Catholic tradition and have a grasp of what their commitment as priests will entail; "most theologates would be delighted to find one-third or even one-fourth of all their students with this profile."[16]

Second, a large group, at least one-third of the total, has recently undergone a conversion or reconversion experience. Many have been away from the church for a number of years. Rather than being rooted in a local church or diocese, they often report choosing a diocese because of a preference for a particular bishop's style or ideology. More than conservative, they are often insecure and so tend to be rigid, overly scrupulous, and fearful.

A third group, perhaps one-fifth of the total, is comprised of students who have been formally identified as Catholics but inconsistent in their practice. Without earlier Catholic education, they have little sense of liturgy or experience in prayer. Some make a successful transition, and having discovered a genuine faith themselves can be successful in help-

---

[13] See Katarina Schuth, *Reasons for the Hope: the Future of Roman Catholic Theologates* (Wilmington, DE: Michael Glazier, 1989) 118.

[14] Schuth, Seminaries, *Theologates, and the Future of Ministry* (Collegeville, MN: Liturgical Press, 1999) 66–67.

[15] Ibid., 67, citing William V. D'Antonio, et al., *Laity American and Catholic: Transforming the Church* (Kansas City, MO: Sheed and Ward, 1996) 87–88.

[16] Schuth, *Seminaries, Theologates,* 75.

ing parishioners struggling with their own faith questions. Others never quite find their way and leave.

Those in the fourth group have a rigid understanding of their faith. Until his death they were unswerving in their devotion to Pope John Paul II, the only pope they had every known. Though they have been immersed in American culture growing up, they now tend to condemn the world as they see it. Seminaries are appreciated as bastions of security. They resist change, avoid critical thought, usually lack a sense of humor, and are drawn to defensive and fundamentalist positions. Some report faculty members they judge to be heterodox to Church authorities. Though quite small, this group has had a disproportionate impact.[17]

Thus, while the majority of seminarians today are not rigid neo-conservatives, many of them are unfamiliar with the basics of their faith and more traditional in their practice. Schuth notes that the low academic quality of many candidates forces faculty to "water down" their courses, waste class time giving quizzes to ensure that they do the reading, and invest their energies in correcting grammar, spelling, and logic in poorly written papers.[18]

What accounts for this more traditional bent of many seminarians and young religious today? A 1992 study of seminary faculty perceptions reported that the "majority of faculty agree that the background of today's seminarian differs from the background of seminarians five to ten years ago. The major differences revolve around dysfunctional backgrounds, not growing up in a Catholic culture, and being more conservative."[19]

One explanation for their conservative attitudes has been that such candidates are fragile psychologically, in need of a highly structured way of life, and may be drawn to the priesthood precisely because it offers both status and security. But there may be other, perhaps more valid explanations. The loss of the culture of Catholicism and theological illiteracy of so many young Catholics, as we saw earlier, means a diminished Catholic identity. Many religious communities have noted this problem in their candidates, and have had to provide courses in basic Catholic doctrine for their novices, even when they have been actively

---

[17] Ibid., 75–79.

[18] Ibid., 93–94.

[19] "A Study of Faculty Perceptions on the Readiness of Seminarians," in *Seminarians in the Nineties: A National Study of Seminarians in Theology*, NCEA (1993) 77.

involved in a Catholic parish, campus community, or social ministry prior to their entrance.

A number of commentators have called attention to the differences between these seminarians and young religious and those charged with their formation. Victor Klimoski argues that they "are not like us." He observes that more and more students lack a grounding in the Catholic tradition, and that their demand for "what the Church teaches" may reflect a quest for stability rather than intellectual shallowness.[20]

Robert Schreiter cautions that those in formation need to be aware of their own bias when they describe younger candidates for religious life as "conservative." He points out that these *formatores* came of age during the 1960s and early 1970s, influenced by the council and the cultural upheaval of the late 1960s. For many of today's candidates, however, "all that they have experienced religiously and in other dimensions of their lives has been discontinuity and fragmentation." Their "conservatism" may actually represent a search for coherence and community: "Wearing the religious habit, engaging in certain exercises of prayer, concern for liturgical correctness, establishing a horarium—all of these are practices that create this kind of identity. These people are largely innocent of the ideological battles of a generation ago." Middle age candidates, on the other hand, may be attempting to return to remembered religious patterns of their childhood.[21]

To better understand the representatives of this emerging generation it helps to consider how their experience differs from that of an earlier generation. The defining moment for Vatican II Catholics was the Second Vatican Council itself. Having been formed in a closed Catholicism and a deductive, apologetic theology, they were delighted to learn that they didn't have to have an answer for every question. They welcomed a less triumphal, more open Church and the opportunity to explore new issues. Some of us well over fifty have probably forgotten how moved we were by *Gaudium et spes*, with its call to dialogue with the modern world, and most of us ultimately embraced the progressive, liberal agenda, which we continue to pursue.

The experience of many seminarians today, however, is completely different. Most of them were born long after the council ended. The only

[20] Victor Klimoski, "Teaching a New Generation," *Seminary Journal* 1/1 (1995) 3–4.

[21] Robert Schreiter, "Reflecting on Religious Life's Future," *Origins* 28/10 (1998) 167.

Church they have known is the post–Vatican II Church, in all its diversity and even confusion. Unlike an older generation, raised on the *Baltimore Catechism*, they complain that they have not really been told what Catholics believe; nor have they been offered a coherent, articulate vision of their faith. They feel this as a loss; they are at a disadvantage with others, better informed, and want to get closer to our Catholic heritage. Their desire to know the great tradition of the Church is one of the reasons that many find the "new apologists" as well as the *Catechism of the Catholic Church* so helpful.

These may be some of the reasons for their apparent conservatism. They are not all fundamentalists or "restorationists." For many of them, their defining experience is coming to the faith at some point in their adult life. Or they have felt the influence of a vibrant evangelicalism in a Catholic form, which makes the reconstructionist, liberal agenda of the Vatican II generation far less appealing. They are less interested in exploring new questions when so many of those they grew up with have no faith at all. Having made at least a tentative commitment to a priesthood which is widely perceived as under attack, they are less likely to be comfortable with ambiguity about what they see as their vocation or place in the Church. Many have a strong desire for ministry, particularly with disadvantaged groups and minorities.

These same tensions are evident in many seminary communities today, where these generational differences are lived out. While seminary faculty members are generally supportive of a more progressive Church agenda, their students are often more conservative, more concerned with questions of Catholic faith, Catholic institutional identity, and evangelization. We mentioned earlier Monika Hellwig's comment that those in ministry programs and seminaries often lack a common theological language, and a common groundedness in the Catholic tradition.[22] Those who teach in seminaries need to be sensitive to these realities and to the generational differences they reflect. As one seminary rector said to me, "for those of us who lived through the council, theologians were our heroes; for many of our seminarians today, theologians are seen as the enemy." Another said that in our professionalization as theologians, we need to make sure we haven't been so "captured" by the academy that we are reluctant to talk about our own faith with our students.

---

[22] Hellwig, "Theology and Catholic Universities: The Situation and Its Possibilities," *Origins* 32/43 (2003) 707.

Younger Catholic Theologians

What about the next generation of Catholic theologians? Are their concerns changing? For some time I've had the impression that the concerns of my own generation of theologians were different, perhaps considerably, from those of younger Catholics in the academy today. A number of things have led to this impression. First of all, many younger theologians approach theology much more intentionally as an ecclesial discipline, not just an academic one. They want to do theology in service to the Church. They are more positive toward the Church, not uncritical, but certainly less angry.

In part their distinction between an ecclesial theology and a simply academic theology may be a reaction to the postmodernist culture that reigns in the academy today. Recently a department I'm familiar with was unable to complete a search for a New Testament theologian because none of the candidates were really interested in the *theology* of the New Testament. One was interested in a feminist interpretation of the New Testament, another approached it from the perspective of gay rights, a third was more concerned with the Greco-Roman context, still another with a post-colonial critique, and so on. This came home to me in a letter from a former student, now a graduate student in economics. She wrote that she was adjusting well to her studies, "although I could do without that post-modernist theory they've been barraging me with. Apparently, there's no such thing as truth, reality, passion, objectivity, etc." Young people like this are much more sympathetic to the warning Cardinal Ratzinger gave about a "dictatorship of relativism," shortly before his election as Benedict XVI.[23]

Another factor in the different approach of many younger theologians today is that a remarkable number of them, some of them very distinguished, have had the Catholic equivalent of a "born again" experience. Having drifted away from Catholicism or joined an evangelical community in their youth, many have had the experience of rediscovering the catholicity of primitive Christianity, with its liturgical, sacramental, and Marian tradition through their reading of the Church fathers or studies of Church history. Having rediscovered their Catholic faith, they have returned to the Church with a new enthusiasm and affection. Because they have some apologetic interests, they are familiar with the works of Catholic writers like Karl Keating, Peter Kreeft, Thomas Howard, Scott

---

[23] Joseph Ratzinger, Homily for Mass opening the conclave (April 18, 2005); *Origins* 34/45 (2005) 719–20.

Hahn, Patrick Madrid, and Mark Shea—the "new apologists" who are enormously popular with many more conservative Catholics.[24]

Like the apologists that my generation read in college, many of these new apologists are converts to the faith. These younger Catholic theologians find their stories not so different from their own. They recognize that they are addressing some very real needs of a considerable number of Catholics today, concerns not often addressed by those theologians whose primary audience is the academy. A number of colleagues have confirmed to me that their graduate students are familiar with these "conservative" authors, while their own colleagues in the academy are not.

Finally, coming again to faith from the indifference and secularism of contemporary culture has also given these young theologians some evangelical interests. Like the seminarians and young religious we considered earlier, the defining movement of their lives was not the council's new vision of freedom and promise of reform, but the experience of discovering a vital faith that has enriched their lives. They want to share the faith with others. They do not find the same evangelical concern among many of their peers in the academy, in spite of the great efforts of Pope John Paul II since the beginning of his pontificate to call the Church to a greater sense of its evangelical mission. So the gap in experience between Catholics of my generation and those who have come on the scene several decades later is considerable. It is a gap in experience that leads to some very real attitudinal differences.

Here are some examples. One comes from a two-part story in the *National Catholic Reporter* about two religious women, one in her fifties, the other in her thirties. The older woman, Sister Carolyn Osiek, was then a professor of New Testament at the Catholic Theological Union in Chicago. She observed that many sisters in her age group seem entrenched in "patterns of life that are based not on the embrace of the future but on the rejection of the past." For many, anger was a common emotion, anger with the Church for not changing as they had hoped, anger at God for getting them into this situation, and anger at the next generation for wanting forms and ways of thinking that they had rejected.

The younger woman, a doctoral student in biblical studies at the University of Chicago, recounted being told by an older sister in her community, "You're not honoring my anger," when one of her peers asked

---

[24] Thomas P. Rausch, *Reconciling Faith and Reason: Apologists, Evangelists, and Theologians in a Divided Church* (Collegeville, MN: Liturgical Press, 2000) 35–52; also Richard Gaillardetz, "Do We Need a New(er) Apologetics?" *America* 190/3 (2004) 26–33.

why some of the older sisters were estranged from the Church and sometimes chose not to attend Mass at the local parish. She added: "On other
occasions, my peers and I in religious life have felt uncomfortable because we happily participate in our local parish. Some sisters have encouraged me to participate in more inclusive liturgies elsewhere. When
we respond that we like our parish, we are often left to feel somehow
less a feminist."[25]

Another example comes from an interview with Dr. Frederick Bauerschmidt, a faculty member at Loyola College, Baltimore, then in his early
forties. A convert to the Church when he was twenty, Bauerschmidt
relates a crisis of faith while in graduate school, which he resolved by
simply continuing to go to church and riding out the storm. Had he
stopped practicing, he says, he wouldn't be a Christian today.

Bauerschmidt says that theology today is incredibly fragmented,

> with Catholics who think that liberation theology in its myriad forms
> (Mestizo, Asian African, feminist, womanist and so on) is still the
> way forward. Others, especially some younger theologians, prefer
> what might broadly be called *ressourcement*. Radical Orthodoxy, one
> variety of *ressourcement*, is distinctive in the directness with which
> it engages with postmodern, post-Nietzschean thought. I suppose
> this is more or less where I fit.

But he also recognizes that for some in the *ressourcement* revival, there is
a tendency to see any criticism of the Church as disloyalty to the Church,
or to facilely dismiss the theology of liberation. He hopes that ultimately
a consistently and constructively critical theological voice will emerge.[26]

Another example comes from Christopher Ruddy, a young theologian
at the University of St. Thomas in St. Paul. He argues that most theologians today take the academy as their primary model; they adopt the
rhetoric of academic freedom, but use it negatively, largely in terms of
freedom *from* interference rather than freedom *for* inquiry and truth. The
result is that

> theology today is often simply nonecclesial and irrelevant to the
> needs of church and society. Answering first to the academy and
> second (perhaps) to the church, many theologians have become

---

[25] "Two Women, a generation apart, view religious life today," *National Catholic
Reporter* (February 18, 2000) 22–23 at 23.

[26] "Can mystics matter? Frederick Bauerschmidt investigates intersection of Christianity and modernity," *National Catholic Reporter* (February 1, 2002) 12–13.

concerned primarily with addressing other scholars, speaking a shorthand unintelligible outside the academy, and piling up increasingly myopic and arcane publications, all for the sake of gaining tenure and promotion.

He laments the fact that many theologians under fifty, under pressure to publish in peer-reviewed journals, are not part of the larger public debate in the Church.[27]

Other examples might include David Nantais' lament that many young Catholics are so poorly educated in their faith and its traditions that they have no way of distinguishing themselves as part of a unique spiritual community.[28] Mark Massa's recent conference at Fordham examining anti-Catholicism is a sign of a new interest in Catholicism by a younger theologian. And finally Grant Kaplan, who in a retrospective on his days at Boston College, notes that he went there as the skeptical product of a secular high school. But once at BC, largely through his friendship with a theology professor who was a priest of the then very troubled Archdiocese of Boston, he went on to "discover the richness of the Catholic tradition, from its art to its great intellectual tradition, to the beautiful witness of its martyrs." The result was a conversion of life; he switched from being a pro-choice Californian to a pro-life Catholic, started going to daily Mass, joined a lay Catholic community, traded a prospective career in law for a doctorate in theology, and now teaches at Loyola of New Orleans.[29]

Converts and Reverts

In addition to these representatives of a new generation of young Catholics, more passionate about their faith, the Catholic Church continues to attract new members, both converts and reverts. In 2000 the *Boston Globe* reported online that the number of adult converts to Catholicism was up by 10 percent.[30] Indeed the Catholic Church is growing on all continents except Europe. Many entering the church are converts

---

[27] Christopher Ruddy, "Young Theologians: Between a Rock and a Hard Place," *Commonweal* 37/8 (April 21, 2000) 17–18 at 18.

[28] David E. Nantais, "Retro-Catholicism," *America* 186 (May 20, 2002) 16–18.

[29] Grant Kaplan, "Remembering Boston," *Conversations on Jesuit Higher Education* 27 (Spring 2005) 48.

[30] *The Boston Globe* (April 23, 2000).

from evangelical Protestantism, among them "new apologists" mentioned earlier like Thomas Howard, Peter Kreeft, Scott and Kimberly Hahn, Marcus Grodi, and Mark Shea.[31]

Hahn, a former Protestant minister, is doing significant theological work. A popular speaker, he has recorded hundreds of tapes and has written ten best-selling books. Grodi, a former evangelical Protestant, began the Coming Home Network in 1993, a ministry directed toward Protestant clergy that has assisted hundreds of non-Catholics in entering the Catholic Church, and is currently assisting several hundred ministers who are still on the journey to full communion with the Church. Mark Shea, also a former evangelical, is now a popular writer and speaker.

Scot McKnight, after interviewing thirty evangelicals who became Catholic, pointed to four principle causes behind their conversions: certainty instead of Protestantism's biblical, theological, and ecclesial pluralism; history, which so often shows that the early Christian writings were Catholic; unity in faith and worship against the multiplication of denominations; and a principle of authority, against the personal interpretation of Scripture.[32]

Some of the new apologists are "reverts," former Catholics who returned to the Catholic Church after joining other churches. Jeff Cavins served for twelve years as a Protestant pastor before returning. Keith Fournier recovered his Catholic faith after becoming involved with evangelical and Pentecostal Protestantism. He is now a constitutional lawyer, ecumenist, and a deacon. Some like Patrick Madrid were raised Catholic but experienced a reawakening or reconversion to their faith as young adults.[33]

Conclusion

If many young Catholics today are poorly informed about their Catholic identity, less committed to the Church as an institution, and reluctant to share their faith with others, there is a significant minority among

---

[31] Mark A. Noll and Carolyn Nystrom profile some of these converts in *Is the Reformation Over? An Evangelical Assessment of Contemporary Roman Catholicism* (Grand Rapids, MI: Baker Academic, 2005) 200–05.

[32] Scot McKnight, "From Wheaton to Rome: Why Evangelicals Become Roman Catholic," *Journal of the Evangelical Theological Society* 45 (September 2002) 462–70.

[33] See Patrick Madrid (ed.), *Surprised by Truth 2* (Manchester, NH: Sophia Institute Press, 2000) 153–81.

them who are passionate about being Catholic, involved in the life of the Church, and eager to present the unique claims of Catholic Christianity to others. Portier calls them evangelical Catholics.

These young people, many of whom have had the Catholic equivalent of a "born again" experience, are often enthused by their discovery or rediscovery of the Church. But many of them, lacking a strong background in the faith, find themselves drawn to more conservative teachers and apologists who don't hesitate to tell them who they are as Catholics and make the case for the uniqueness of their Church, something many mainstream Catholic theologians seem reluctant to do. We will return to the new apologists in the final chapter.

There are also some encouraging signs of younger Catholics and evangelicals working together and learning from each other that may give another sense to "evangelical Catholics." For example, Catholics and Evangelicals are working together in the Campus Ministry programs at two Catholic schools, the University of San Diego and Lewis University outside Chicago. In 2004 I attended a meeting at Lewis University, "Common Ground II: Gifts We Bring to the Table," really a follow-up to an earlier meeting of representatives of InterVarsity Fellowship and Catholic campus ministers held at the University of San Diego in January 2001.

Nor are the young adults, seminarians, and theologians we have considered here the only ones showing a new enthusiasm for Catholicism. The Church continues to draw new members, many of them converts from evangelical Protestantism who bring their evangelical outreach to their new ecclesial home. The World Wide Web has a plethora of sites sponsored by a new generation of apologists and evangelists, many of whom are converts themselves.

Thus, if many young adult Catholics today have a diminished commitment to their Church as an institution and are unfamiliar with Catholicism's core narratives and tradition, there are also signs of others among them much better informed about their faith and enthusiastic about their Church. Their energy and intelligence suggest that these "evangelical Catholics" will play an important role in the Catholicism of tomorrow.

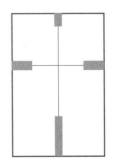

Chapter 7

Some Concluding Reflections

In this book we have been concerned with questions of Catholic identity, particularly the identity of young Catholics who will make up the Church's future generations. In this final chapter I'd like to explore some of the issues these questions raise, among them the question of an authentic spirituality, the implications for the way authority is exercised in what has become a church of choice, the strengths and weaknesses of the new apologists' approach to Catholic identity, and the question of the uniqueness of Catholicism. Finally, I'll attempt to draw some more general conclusions.

Spiritual but not Religious

The modern tendency to speak of spirituality without reference to religion is problematic for a number of reasons. First of all, the claim, "I'm spiritual but not religious" usually means that faith, belief, and practice are all matters of personal choice, without accountability to any mediating community of faith.

While social scientists have noted the tendency to separate spirituality and religion, some of them are beginning to raise critical questions about the depth of the current interest in spirituality. Princeton's Robert Wuthnow, one of the premiere sociologists of religion in the U.S. today, writes that "The idea that spirituality is being pursued outside of organized religion is both plausible and worrisome."[1] He wonders how

---

[1] Robert Wuthnow, *All in Sync; How Music and Art Are Revitalizing American Religion* (Berkeley: University of California Press, 2003) 32.

surveys can effectively measure people's interest in spirituality when spirituality itself can mean so many different things. Much of it seems irrational, based on self-indulgent fantasizing, or essentially private, personally-invented sets of beliefs and practices. When books like *Chicken Soup for the Soul* and *The Celestine Prophecy* pass for spirituality, serious-minded observers of American religion are concerned "because they provide ready-made answers for the small setbacks and petty anxieties of ordinary life but do not speak of a righteous God who demands any thing of believers."[2] Too seldom does such interest in spirituality translate into action. As we saw in Chapter 1, the authors of the UNC study describe such a subjective, individualistic approach to religion as "Moralistic Therapeutic Deism."[3]

This tendency to define spirituality on the basis of subjective feelings or personal preference, without service of others or engagement in a community of faith that might provide an external check remains problematic. Wuthnow notes that among those who say that spirituality is fairly important, three-quarters do not attend religious services regularly and half are not church members. The implication here is that some questions could be raised about the seriousness of their spiritual commitment. He argues that "people with the highest commitment to spiritual growth are overwhelmingly involved in religious organizations: eighty percent of those who value spiritual growth the most are church members, and seventy-one percent say they attend worship services almost every week."[4]

From a theological perspective, the tendency to construct one's beliefs, practices, and spirituality without the help of a community mediating a received religious tradition is suspect. Behind this tendency to self-sufficiency lies the autonomous self, the person who is accountable to no authority outside his or her ego—not to the Scripture, not to creed or cult, not even to God. In matters religious the self is absolute. The sovereign ego rules. As the sage said, "whoever seeks to be his own master becomes the disciple of a fool."

[2] Wuthnow, *All in Sync*, 24–25 at 25.

[3] Christian Smith and Melinda Lundquist Denton, *Soul Searching: The Religious and Spiritual Lives of American Teenagers* (New York: Oxford University Press, 2005) 162–63.

[4] Wuthnow, *All in Sync*, 36; Penny Marler and Kirk Hadaway reach a similar conclusion in "Being Religious and Being Spiritual in America: A Zero-Sum Proposition?" *The Journal for the Scientific Study of Religion*, 41/2 (June 2002) 297.

In fact, warnings against this kind of extreme self-reliance are made directly in the Scriptures. The story of the fall in the opening chapters of the book of Genesis addresses this tendency; here the serpent seduces the first man and woman with the promise that if they eat of the forbidden fruit, their eyes will be opened and they will become like gods themselves, knowing what is good and what is evil (Gen 3:5). The temptation is attractive, and has the appearance of a good. But in reality it represents the classic "I will not serve." In trying to claim equality with their creator, usurping God's rightful place, the man and woman overturn the order of creation, with disastrous effects. They are alienated from God, from nature, and from themselves. The results are tragic. First is fratricide, with Cain killing his brother Abel. Then the story of the great flood illustrates how the lawlessness and evil of mortals almost brings about the destruction of the earth itself—not God's doing but their own. Finally, the story of the Tower of Babel shows how human pride and arrogance result in a further alienation of the human family through the confusing of their language, scattering them over the face of the earth without any hope of community.

The modern "turn towards the subject," the intellectual revolution begun by Descartes (1596–1650) and continued by Locke, Hume, Kant, Hegel, and Feuerbach can be seen as a philosophical expression of this tendency to make the human person the center and measure of all things. Friedrich Nietzsche (1844–1900) goes so far as to say that humans had willed the death of God; they had killed him, a dramatic way of saying that modern culture had made God irrelevant.[5] In the new world that resulted, values could not be imposed but only chosen, created by the "superman" who lived beyond good and evil.

From a practical perspective, modernity's autonomous self leads either to atheism or to idolatry. The autonomous self by definition cannot afford to recognize a divine Other, the Absolute before whom the religious man or woman falls in reverence and awe. The very idea of such heteronomy or submission to another is offensive; it means that the self is no longer sovereign. Kilian McDonnell has pointed to the rejection of heteronomy as a problematic aspect of some contemporary feminist Christologies. Since Christology necessarily involves heteronomy, "radical autonomy is radical feminism's other name."[6] He points to the feminist objection

---

[5] Friedrich Nietzsche, *The Gay Science*, ed. Bernard Williams (Cambridge: Cambridge University Press, 2001) (no. 125) 119–20.

[6] See Kilian McDonnell, "Feminist Mariologies: Heteronomy / Subordination and the Scandal of Christology," *Theological Studies* 66/3 (September 2005) 532.

that Luke's portrayal of Mary in the Annunciation as *doulē*, that is "hand-maid," "servant," or "female slave," belongs to the patriarchal form of heteronomy. Countering this, he calls to mind the Old Testament custom of identifying great figures in salvation history as "slaves" of Yahweh, for example, Moses (2 Kings 18:12), Joshua (Judges 2:8), Abraham (Psalm 105:42), and the prophets (Amos 3:7; Zech 1:6). Luke locates Mary among these figures.[7] Citing the story of Jesus in the gospels McDonnell observes, "Heteronomy and submission of some kind seem to belong to the interior life of God."[8]

Sometimes the self seeks to remain autonomous by creating its own god. How often have we heard someone say that he or she is searching for "a God I am comfortable with," "a God who is always there for me," a God who does not make demands. However such a God is often con-structed out of sentimentality or the ideas of popular culture. It is not the God of the biblical tradition, the God who commands Moses, "Re-move the sandals from your feet, for the place where you stand is holy ground" (Exod 3:5). Such a God is not the God of Jesus. With his hard sayings, Jesus calls for a *metanoia* or conversion; he tells us "how narrow the gate and constricted the road that leads to life" (Matt 7:13). He says "Not everyone who says to me, 'Lord, Lord,' will enter the kingdom of heaven, but only the one who does the will of my Father in heaven" (Matt 7:21). This is the Jesus who says repeatedly "Whoever wishes to come after me must deny himself, take up his cross, and follow me" (Mark 8:34) or again, the seed must fall into the ground and die if it is to bring forth fruit (John 12:24).

Authority in a Church of Choice

If many young adult Catholics are constructing their own religious identity as Hoge argues, thus transforming the Catholic Church "from a perceived church of obligation and obedience to a church of choice,"[9] what are the implications of this transformation for the Church? What is increasingly evident is the need for renewal and reform in the Church's

---

[7] Ibid., 533.

[8] Ibid., 535.

[9] Dean R. Hoge, William D. Dinges, Mary Johnson, Juan L. Gonzales, Jr., *Young Adult Catholics: Religion in the Culture of Choice* (Notre Dame, IN: University of Notre Dame Press, 2001) 225.

structures of authority, that is, for significant change in its decision-making processes. Clearly the post–Vatican II generations are asking for this.

According to William D'Antonio and associates, 64 percent of post–Vatican II Catholics believe that the Church should be governed democratically at every level—parish, diocesan, and the Vatican; 83 percent think that the laity should be involved in choosing their priests, and 69 percent believe that they should be consulted about the ordination of women.[10]

Hoge and his associates said that the largest type in their sample were young adult Catholics who are all but indistinguishable from mainline Protestants. Disinclined to define themselves in terms of institutional standards, "they want a more egalitarian, participatory, and democratic Church."[11] At the end of their study they asked the young adults, "What if you had a chance to address the American Catholic bishops. . . . What would you say" (230).

The first response the researchers heard was that the Church "should be more welcoming to young adults, more willing to address issues and concerns relevant to them, and more willing to listen seriously to them instead of issuing authoritative pronouncements or asserting that issues are closed and cannot be discussed" (231). Many young adults do not see any connection between what the Church teaches and divine law, particularly concerning issues dealing with sexuality. Some decide these questions on the basis of cultural values and feel that what is right is what is right for them. Others argue that they are following their conscience, making the best judgment possible in their circumstances.

I point this out, not to argue that they are necessarily right. But if the Church really wants to speak to young adults today, it must recognize how deficient is its own credibility. Most young Catholics do not believe that a matter is resolved simply because authority has pronounced on it.

Furthermore, young adults are not the only ones calling for renewal and reform in the Catholic Church today. Many theologians and bishops have sought to address these issues. Retired San Francisco Archbishop John Quinn in an address at Oxford University in 1996 called for a wider and more serious consultation with bishops and episcopal conferences on a number of "grave questions" that have been closed to discussion, for a "true, active collegiality and not merely a passive collegiality," for

---

[10] D'Antonio, et al., *Laity, American and Catholic: Transforming the Church* (Kansas City, MO: Sheed and Ward, 1996) 74.

[11] Hoge, *Young Adult Catholics*, 223.

a greater involvement of local churches in the selection of bishops, and for the implementation within the Church of the principle of subsidiarity, allowing local decisions to be made at local levels rather than by higher authorities.[12] Cardinal Walter Kasper has made similar comments, pointing out that "Many laypersons and priests can no longer understand universal church regulations, and simply ignore them. This applies both to ethical issues and to questions of sacramental and ecumenical praxis, such as the admission of divorced and remarried persons to communion or the offer of eucharistic hospitality to non-Catholics."[13] And other members of the hierarchy have begun to speak out.[14]

The problem is not so much structural as it is pastoral; it concerns the way that authority is exercised. The Second Vatican Council replaced a monarchical theology of authority and governance with a collegial theology of the episcopal office, but the years after the council have witnessed a recentering of authority and decision-making power in Rome. This has meant that power and authority rest, not primarily with the bishops and pope acting together, but with the Roman curia. As theologian Richard Gaillardetz points out, the distinction between the pope and bishops as legislators for the church and the curial dicasteries as executors has been ignored, "with the result that the congregations of the Roman curia have virtually replaced the college of bishops as the principal legislators of the Church."[15]

A further problem is that lay Catholics have little say in the Church's decision-making process, either in Rome or at the level of the local church. Nothing has brought this problem home more clearly than the sexual abuse scandal in the United States. More and more laypeople are becoming aware that there are no institutional checks and balances that allow them some say about how authority is exercised in the Church. They have no way to address the problem of an incompetent pastor or an authoritarian bishop, no say over their appointment, no way to bring their own concerns and experience to the decision-making process of the universal Church. There are no structures of accountability. Lay

[12] John R. Quinn, "Considering the Papacy," *Origins* 26/8 (July 18, 1996) 121–25 at 123.

[13] Walter Kasper, *Leadership in the Church: How Traditional Roles Can Serve the Christian Community Today*, trans. Brian McNeil (New York: Crossroad, 2003) 159.

[14] Kilian McDonnell in "Our Dysfunctional Church," *The Tablet* 225/8 (Sept. 8, 2001), 1661.

[15] Richard Gaillardetz, *Teaching With Authority: A Theology of the Magisterium in the Church* (Collegeville, MN: Liturgical Press, 1997) 287.

Catholics are increasingly seeing the present crisis as calling them to adult status in the life of the church.[16]

According to the Dogmatic Constitution on the Church, "To the extent of their knowledge, competence or authority the laity are entitled, and indeed sometimes duty-bound, to express their opinion on matters which concern the good of the church" (LG 37). But for too many Catholics the only dialogue in the Church seems to be a dialogue with the deaf. Those in authority don't really listen to representatives of the laity who are sometimes more competent in areas such as theology, pastoral ministry, religious education, family life and sexuality, and the political dynamics that surround issues of social justice. Too often they forbid discussion of controverted issues, overturn decisions of episcopal conferences, and raise new barriers to sharing biblical texts or prayers with other Christians.[17] Furthermore, the bishops are frequently unwilling to press Roman authorities to address unresolved problems or to challenge them when they ignore or overrule their decisions. The result is a further loss of episcopal credibility.

There are too many issues like birth control, questions in sexuality, women's role in the Church, biomedical ethics, and end of life issues that are answered with instructions from Vatican congregations without consultation of others with professional competence. The bishops themselves have not had a genuine dialogue on these issues. Many of them are relatively new issues not addressed by the tradition, or addressed only inadequately. The danger is that too many Catholics will simply circumscribe the area of their involvement, limiting it to their local parish community, depriving the larger church for which they are co-responsible of their energy and expertise.

Thus young Catholics are not the only ones calling for consultation, dialogue, and a willingness to confront difficult issues. This is not to argue for deciding doctrine by majority vote, overturning the Church's papal-episcopal structure. But the fact is that most Catholics no longer identify the hierarchy's voice with God's. Their compliance is no longer a given, except in the narrow area of the Church's sacramental life where

---

[16] See Francis Oakley and Bruce Russett, ed. *Governance, Accountability, and the Future of the Catholic Church* (New York: Continuum, 2004); also Thomas P. Rausch "The Lay Vocation and Voice of the Faithful," *America* 189/9 (September 29, 2003) 8–11.

[17] See Mark R. Francis, "The Call for Eucharistic Renewal in a Multi-Cultural World," *Centro Pro Unione* 68 (Fall 2005) 7–14; also John Wilkins, "Lost in Translation: The Bishops, the Vatican and the English Liturgy," *Commonweal* 132/21 (December 2, 2005) 13–20.

they have little choice.[18] If, as Roger Haight observes, even the Catholic Church has become a voluntary organization to which people freely commit to belong, "will not church authority have to involve dialogue and consent as in a congregational or free church polity"?[19]

Catholic Identity and the New Apologists

If some contemporary Catholics are eager for renewal and reform in the way their Church makes decisions, the great popularity of the "new apologists" is evidence of a genuine need on the part of many Catholics in the United States today for a renewed sense of Catholic identity. Many of these apologists are converts from evangelical Protestantism as we have seen. Concerned to help Catholics respond to proselytizing efforts by conservative Protestants and to strengthen their Catholic identity, they sponsor a host of print and online ministries, prominent among them Karl Keating's *Catholic Answers* and Patrick Madrid's *Envoy* Magazine.

I've been critical of the new apologists' approach to apologetics and catechesis.[20] Too often they reflect a literalist, noncritical biblicism, an often simplistic appeal to the biblical text which constructs whole theologies on metaphors or single verses. Important as Scripture is, for Catholics revelation is not primarily a biblical text, a magisterial pronouncement, or a theology, but a person, Jesus the Christ. Similarly, the new apologists' approach to doctrine is often nonhistorical; it shows little appreciation for historical context, development, and even change. Difficult questions such as the development of the papacy are not answered simply by quoting one or two biblical texts or the *Catechism of the Catholic Church*. A precritical approach does not help Catholics to enter into dialogue with modernity. The new apologists' attitude toward other Christian communities is often anti-Protestant and triumphal rather than reflecting the ecumenical sensitivity called for by the Second Vatican Council.

At the same time, in recent years I've become more sympathetic to some of the concerns of the new apologists. Their popularity is evidence

---

[18] Andrew M. Greeley, *The Catholic Revolution* (Berkeley: University of California Press, 2004) 168–71.

[19] Roger Haight, *Christian Community in History:* Vol. I: *Historical Ecclesiology* (New York: Continuum, 2004) 34.

[20] Thomas P. Rausch, *Reconciling Faith and Reason: Apologists, Evangelists, and Theologians in a Divided Church* (Collegeville, MN: Liturgical Press, 2000) 39–52.

that that they are addressing some real needs of contemporary Catholics, particularly their "thin" sense of their Catholic identity and their inability to respond adequately when challenged by more polemical Protestants. Clearly they have helped many Catholics to rediscover the biblical and historical foundations for their faith and given them greater confidence in the face of those who attack it.

Richard Gaillardetz lauds the new apologists for their zeal. They are enthusiastic about their faith, even passionate about it, and are not afraid to talk about doctrine.[21] This is refreshing. Yet his support is not without qualification. He makes the perceptive observation that while their "doctrinal orthodoxy as Catholics may be unimpeachable . . . their deeper theological imagination often remains strikingly Protestant."[22] Important as a strong and viable Catholic identity is, it cannot be built on a foundation that is precritical, ignorant of history, anti-intellectual and anti-ecumenical. Gaillardetz argues that an adequate Catholic identity must be based on five imperatives.[23] First, the "catechetical imperative" demands that catechesis must cultivate the Catholic imagination in its incarnational, eucharistic, Petrine, sacramental, and Marian richness. But to do this it must be historically conscious; it cannot ignore the history and development of Catholic doctrine.

Second, given the individualistic tendencies of young evangelical Catholics (and other young Catholics), the communal imperative recognizes the need to respond to a weakened sense of ecclesial and communal identity by offering these Catholics small faith-sharing communities or parish renewal programs. They need to deepen their faith by exploring it with others who are engaged with both the whole Church and the wider world.

Third, a Catholic identity cannot ignore the ecumenical imperative if it is to be faithful to the Second Vatican Council's commitment to the cause of reconciliation and Christian unity. That excludes a simplistic "ecumenism of return." The Council taught that all ecumenism begins with conversion, with a change of heart (UR 7).[24] Nor can ecumenism be

---

[21] Richard Gaillardetz, "Do We Need a New(er) Apologetics?" *America* 190/3 (2004) 27.

[22] Gaillardetz, "Apologetics, Evangelization and Ecumenism Today," *Origins* 35/1 (2005) 12.

[23] For what follows see Gaillardetz, "Apologetics, Evangelization and Ecumenism Today," 11–15.

[24] See *The Basic Sixteen Documents of Vatican II*, ed. Austin Flannery (Northport, NY: Costello Publishing, 1996).

reduced to a superficial alliance between the Catholic right and evangelical Christians around abortion, same sex-marriage, and issues associated with the Terri Schiavo case. Such narrow ecumenism, espoused by Catholics like George Weigel and Richard John Neuhaus, does not adequately represent the Council's goal of the full, visible unity of the churches.

Fourth, an evangelical imperative sees apologetics as a moment in a larger work of evangelization and mission. Evangelization is at the heart of the Church's mission, but that mission cannot be reduced to simply making others Catholic. As the Second Vatican Council, the Pontifical Council for Interreligious Dialogue, and Pope John Paul II have all stressed, evangelization involves both proclamation and dialogue with culture and other religions.[25]

Finally, a mystagogical imperative helps Catholics to recognize that God's grace is present, not just in the Church, but also in the world. Church teaching must illumine people's daily lives and bring them into critical conversation with the world today, with culture, including its popular forms, as well as with science and the ethical dilemmas faced by those living in a postmodern world.

The Uniqueness of Catholicism

While researchers like Dean Hoge and James Davidson have noted the weak Catholic identity and diminished institutional commitment of many young Catholics, William Portier's suggestion that more attention should be paid to the 30 percent in Davidson's study (or the 48 percent in Hoge's) who agree that the Catholic Church is the "one true Church" merits further reflection.[26]

Portier recognizes, of course, that questions such as, "is the Catholic Church the one true Church" can be overstated and theologically misleading. But this pride in their Church and sense for its historical uniqueness should not be simply dismissed. What if, Portier asks, post-subculture conditions are giving rise to new kinds of Catholics? These young Catho-

---

[25] See *Nostra aetate* and *Ad gentes* (no. 18); also the Pontifical Council for Interreligious Dialogue, "Dialogue and Proclamation," *Origins* 21/8 (1991) 121–35; also www.vatican.va.

[26] William L. Portier, "Here Come the Evangelical Catholics," *Communio* 31 (Spring 2004) 51–52; see James D. Davidson, *The Search for Common Ground: What Unites and Divides Catholic Americans* (Huntington, IN: Our Sunday Visitor, 1997) 126; Hoge, *Young Adult Catholics*, 57.

lics are enthusiastic about their Church. They are not interested in a "restoration" to a past they never knew, but want to know clearly what it means to be Catholic and how they might explain their ecclesial faith to others. They are concerned about Catholic identity.[27]

Thus the question about the Catholic Church being the true Church needs to be addressed, but in a nuanced way. It should not be treated as some Catholic apologists do, in what Richard Gaillardetz calls "a hermeneutically naïve and ahistorical mode."[28] There needs to be a middle road between the one true church ecclesiology implicit in the latter approach, and the ecclesiological relativism, the one-church-is-as-good-as-another approach characteristic of so many today. At the same time, the Catholic Church has a claim to antiquity, catholicity, and apostolicity that is unique and difficult to deny.

First of all, the Catholic Church (along with the Orthodox churches) rightly claims visible, historical continuity with the earliest Christian churches. From this perspective, the Catholic Church represents the world's oldest institution, with continuity in structure, government, and faith maintained against the vicissitudes of history that is remarkable. Catholics see in this the fulfillment of Jesus' promise to Peter: "you are Peter, and upon this rock I will build my church, and the gates of the netherworld shall not prevail against it" (Matt 16:18). In her wonderful autobiography Dorothy Day, the cofounder of the Catholic Worker movement, tells us that she was drawn to Christianity by her need to love and praise God with other people. When the time came to choose a church she says simply, "Without even looking into the claims of the Catholic Church, I was willing to admit that for me she was the one true Church. She had come down through the centuries since the time of Peter, and far from being dead, she claimed and held the allegiance of the masses of people in all the cities where I had lived."[29]

Second, as Hans Küng has observed, only one church, from the time of Ignatius of Antioch (c. 110) down to the present day, has been known as the "Catholic Church," despite the wish of other churches to be called catholic. He cites Augustine, who addressed this issue in the early fifth century:

---

[27] Ibid., 52–53.

[28] Gaillardetz, "Apologetics, Evangelization and Ecumenism Today," 11.

[29] Dorothy Day, *The Long Loneliness: The Autobiography of Dorothy Day* (Harper-SanFrancisco, 1981) 139.

> . . . the Church possesses precisely the name 'Catholic', a name which significantly and despite all heresies only this one Church has retained, so that, although all heretics would like to think of themselves as Catholic, no heretic would ever dare to answer a stranger's questions as to where 'the Catholics' meet together by pointing to his basilica or his house.[30]

Without suggesting that other, newer churches are "uncatholic communities," Küng argues that all of these churches—Orthodox churches of the East, Lutheran, Reformed, Anglican, and all the churches which have sprung from them—while they do not wish to be considered "new" churches, have found it necessary to distinguish themselves from the Catholic Church and were once directly or indirectly linked with her. "[T]hese daughters, so unlike one another and often so unlike her, are still her children."[31]

Third, the Second Vatican Council takes that middle road between a one true church ecclesiology and ecclesiological relativism which would make all churches equally valid. It teaches that "all the means of salvation" are given to the Catholic Church through Christ "who rules her through the Supreme Pontiff and the bishops. This joining is effected by the bonds of professed faith, of the sacraments, of ecclesiastical government, and of communion" (LG 14). It believes that the Church of Christ "subsists in the Catholic Church, which is governed by the successor of Peter and by the bishops in union with that successor" (LG 8). In other words, the Church of Christ is realized in its essential completeness in the Catholic Church.[32]

At the same time, the Catholic Church recognizes the ecclesial reality of other Christian churches and ecclesial communities (cf. LG 15; UR 3), thus denying that there is an "ecclesial vacuum" outside the Catholic Church,[33] unlike some evangelicals who are reluctant even to recognize Catholics as Christians.

Finally, the Catholic Church has a universality and catholicity that makes it unique. It is present in almost every country. A little over half

[30] Augustine, *De vera religione* 7.12; PL 34, 128; cited by Hans Küng, *The Church* (New York: Sheed and Ward, 1967) 306.

[31] Küng, *The Church*, 307.

[32] Congregation for the Doctrine of the Faith, *Dominus Iesus* (no. 17); *Origins* 30/14 (Sept. 14, 2000) 216.

[33] Kasper, "*Prolusio*," in the Pontifical Council for Promoting Christian Unity *Information Service* 109 (2002/I–II) 18.

of the world's Christians are Catholics, some 53 percent. At the 1985 Extraordinary Synod of Bishops in Rome, 74 percent of the bishops came from countries other than those in Europe or North America. At the 2005 Synod on the Eucharist the 244 bishops present came from some 118 countries. In an era of globalization, in which people around the world are being more closely linked by electronic systems, interconnected economies, and mass culture, the Catholic Church is a world communion with the structures that could link the various Christian churches together into a communion of communions that would be truly catholic.[34] It is already a world church, "the oldest significant globe-oriented organization."[35] With international structures and networks in place, it is uniquely positioned to help world Christianity carry out its evangelical and social mission on a global scale.

Conclusion

What conclusions can we draw from our study of Catholic identity?

1. *Lower Levels of Engagement.* The UNC study found Catholic teenagers *behind* Protestant teenagers by as much as 25 percentage points on various standards of religious belief, practice, experiences, and commitments.[36] The UCLA study on the spiritual life of college students found that Catholics tended to score *below* the overall average on standards for religious commitment and engagement.[37]

2. *Inability to Articulate their Faith.* The study of young adult Catholics by Dean Hoge and his associates indicates that these young adults are not well-versed in the core narratives of their faith, cannot always identify what is distinctive about Catholicism, or articulate a clear Catholic identity. At the end of their study of American teens, the authors of the UNC study observe that while those they studied were quite articulate about drinking, drugs, STDs, and safe sex, all subjects they had been drilled in, they were not able to talk specifically about Jesus. Arguing that inarticulacy undermines the possibilities of reality, they say that a

---

[34] Thomas P. Rausch, *Towards a Truly Catholic Church* (Collegeville, MN: Liturgical Press, 2005).

[35] Roland Robertson, "Religion and the Global Field," *Social Compass* 41 (1994) 129.

[36] Smith and Denton, *Soul Searching*, 194.

[37] www.spirituality.ucla.edu.

major challenge for religious educators seems to be "helping teens to practice talking about their faith, providing practice at using vocabularies, grammars, stories, and key messages of faith." They make the observation that religious education in the U.S. is failing when it comes to preparing youth to articulate their faith.[38]

3. *Diminished Institutional Commitment.* We've also seen that most young adult Catholics lack a strong commitment to the Catholic Church as an institution and are less familiar with the ecclesial dimension of their faith. Most young Catholics see little connection between religion and spirituality and believe that one can be a good Catholic without participating in the liturgical life of the Church. In this the researchers found them little different from mainline Protestants, tending to view Catholicism as one denomination among others.[39] The most reasonable prediction is that the number of those who say that they would never leave the Catholic Church will continue to decline, as the 2005 *NCR* survey suggests. Still, it remains true the church involvement typically increases from the young adult to middle adult years, particularly as young adults begin to have families of their own.[40]

4. *A Significant Minority.* Not all young Catholics today fit the profile we have been describing. While there are some progressive young Catholics fully engaged in their faith, there is also considerable evidence of a significant minority, variously described as evangelical Catholics, neo-conservatives, or John Paul II Catholics who are both strongly ecclesial in their faith and more traditional in its expression. Their life experience is different from Catholics over fifty. So is their agenda. Many have come to a committed Catholic life from nonpracticing families and a secular, postmodernist culture. A considerable number have had a Catholic version of the "born again" experience. They are more concerned with Catholic life and evangelization than with Church reform. The energy and commitment of these young Catholics is an encouraging sign.

Still their potential to advance the Church's mission will be lost if they prove unable to move beyond an uncritical triumphalism or retreat into

---

[38] Smith and Denton, *Soul Searching*, 267–68; see Charles Taylor, *Sources of the Self: the Making of the Modern Identity* (Cambridge, MA: Harvard University Press, 1989).

[39] Hoge, *Young Adult Catholics*, 221–23.

[40] Cf. Dean R. Hoge, in "Attitudes of Catholics Highly Committed to the Church," NCR Survey of U.S. Catholics, *National Catholic Reporter* (September 30, 2005); also John A. Coleman, "Young Adults: A Look at the Demographics," *Commonweal* (September 14, 1990) 483–90.

a new Catholic ghetto. A restoration of the pre–Vatican II Catholic sub-culture is neither possible nor desirable. They need to find common ground with the larger group of young Catholics and with the main-stream Church if they are to realize an authentic catholicity and truly serve the Church.

5. *A Problem of Credibility.* Much of this book has been analytical and de-scriptive. Other commentators will offer a different diagnosis. They would point to a widespread ignorance of Church teaching and discipline, di-minishing mass attendance and religious practice, tolerance of divorce and invalid marriages, "dissenting" theologians, the high number of gay seminarians and priests, and secularized Catholic colleges and universi-ties. But such commentators ignore the fact that the official Church itself has a credibility problem. A centralized authority issues pronouncements on all subjects, but few seem to be listening. Too often there is a discon-nect between the concerns of authority and what troubles the minds and hearts of the faithful. Greeley's metaphor is apt; the old wineskins have broken. Authority, important as it is, must listen as well as teach.

Many young Catholics exhibit a remarkable ability to live with diver-sity in values and lifestyle. They are compassionate and willing to accept those who are different and cannot understand language and attitudes from the official Church they judge to be exclusive or condemnatory. There is ample evidence that the Church has a credibility problem with many of its younger members, particularly in the areas of gender equal-ity and sexuality.[41]

6. *Importance of Parents and Family.* With the loss of a strong Catholic subculture, whatever familiarity with the Catholic tradition young Catholics have will have to come from their homes, particularly from their parents. Indeed, the UNC study of the spiritual life of teenagers says in its conclusion that most teenagers are not alienated or rebellious in regard to religious involvement; "the vast majority are happy simply to accept the one religion in which they were raised."[42] Most are not looking for radically new, postmodern programs and are not seekers claiming to be spiritual but not religious. It is the example of their parents and their involvement in their faith communities that is most significant (267). Of course some children from homes with intelligent and devout parents will choose to go a different way.

---

[41] Hoge, *Young Adult Catholics*, 231.
[42] Smith and Denton, *Soul Searching*, 260.

Still, the evidence for parental influence remains strong. Thus we have stressed the importance of the family as the domestic church, the cradle where faith is nurtured and children are socialized into the tradition. The Christian family is an efficacious sacrament.

The UNC study also emphasized that the Catholic Church needs to "invest a great deal more attention, creativity, and institutional resources into its young members—and therefore into its own life" (217). They need simple, ordinary adult relationships, relationships with mature adults able to take young people seriously, learn their names, show interest in them and their concerns, and work toward becoming models and partners with them (266–69). They also need parishes and pastors that will welcome their energy and creativity.

7. *Catholicism as a Way of Life.* Catholicism is not just a particular church or Christian tradition; it is a way of life, a way of seeing the world, rooted in what we have described as the Catholic sacramental imagination. A Catholic imagination does not restrict God's grace to sacramental symbols and ritual moments. It includes more than the explicitly religious. Because it takes its fundamental inspiration from the doctrine of the incarnation, it recognizes that God's grace is abundantly present in creation and the genuinely human.

Yet it is very different from a sentimental Deism, which posits a benevolent God who makes no demands other than to be "nice" and is always available when needed. Being Catholic means being part of God's people, a disciple of Jesus, and member of his Body, the Church. If the Catholic Church is not the whole of the Church, it has a unique claim to antiquity, catholicity, and apostolicity. Its mission is evangelical; it includes both proclamation and dialogue. Its ministry cannot be narrowly ecclesial. It must reach out to serve the less fortunate and make Christ's healing presence felt in the wider world.

8. *Strategies for Institutional Identity.* Catholic institutions, particularly Catholic colleges and universities, also struggle with how to safeguard and enhance their Catholic identity today. Religious iconography, the centrality of a chapel, a clear mission statement as well as specific strategies such as hiring for mission, spiritual development programs for faculty and staff, presidential assistants or vice-presidents for mission and identity all can be helpful. The growing number of Catholic Studies departments also reflects recognition of the needs of Catholic undergraduates, their lack of familiarity with Catholic theology, doctrine, and culture.

9. *Dialogue and Participation.* There is growing evidence of a sea change taking place in the way contemporary Catholics regard the governance of their Church. An increasing number of young Catholics no longer see their involvement in the life of the Church as a matter of obligation and obedience. Rather the Church has become a voluntary society, a Church of choice, and they want it to be a more egalitarian, participatory, and democratic community.[43] Many Catholics, galvanized by the recent clergy sexual abuse scandal and the failures of authority it revealed, feel themselves called to a more adult role in the Church's life. When the bishop of Regensburg dissolved an elected diocesan council in November 2005, replacing it with an appointed body, he was publicly criticized by the president of the German bishops' conference. In Western Europe, where the vast majority of Catholics are no longer involved in the life of the Church, this kind of unilateral clerical action is no longer acceptable. Even so, lay participation is still very much at the sufferance of the bishop. The Church still needs to negotiate ways to provide for some share in ecclesial decision-making by the laity and greater accountability for its bishops.

Hoge notes that the total U.S. Catholic population is growing at about 10 percent per decade while the number of parishes without a resident priest continues to increase. He estimates that by 2010, the average parish size will be about 3,500. He makes three recommendations. First, don't force parishes to close. Catholics like their parishes. Church authorities should not make these decisions unilaterally, but allow lay people themselves to determine the future of their parishes. Second, support the emerging lay ministries, which will increasingly carry out ordinary, non-sacramental ministry in these parishes. Third, if a parish cannot *be* small, it can at least *act* small, with smaller prayer circles, faith-sharing groups, parenting seminars and other smaller groups, which make possible spiritual growth and meaningful relationships.[44] Most Catholics are not looking for a megachurch.

10. *Signs of Hope.* There is still much life and vitality in the Catholic Church. The number of Catholics is increasing on all continents except Europe. In 2006, roughly 154,000 adults joined the Church through the RCIA. Every year some 40,000 plus people, most of them young, make

---

[43] Cf. Hoge, *Young Adult Catholics,* 223–25; see also D'Antonio, et al., *Laity, American and Catholic: Transforming the Church,* 74.

[44] Reported in *The Tidings* (December 10, 2004).

the trip to Anaheim in Orange County for the Religious Education Congress, sponsored by the Archdiocese of Los Angeles. Most of them are involved in the Church and its ministries. Lay ministries in the U.S. have exploded. There are nearly 31,000 paid lay ministers working in parishes at least 20 hours per week, 80 percent of them women, with a growing percentage of lay ministers coming from minority communities.[45] Salaries for full-time lay ministers have risen substantially. By 2005, the average was $35,261, the median $37,500. We have some wonderful bishops across the country, in spite of Rome's tendency in recent years to seek episcopal appointments known for their *Romanita*.

The Catholic Church has considerable social capital in the United States as the largest single nongovernmental provider of social services. It is the largest operator of private schools; its primary and secondary schools play an important role, particularly for students from poorer families and minority groups. These schools have a lower dropout rate (3.4 percent) than both public (14.4 percent) and other private schools (11.9 percent). And 99 percent of Catholic high school students graduate, with 97 percent going on to some form of postsecondary education. Catholic school students also score well on standardized tests, surpassing standards established by federal and state agencies.[46]

The Catholic Church also has the largest nonprofit health-care system, accounting for 17 percent of all U.S. hospital admissions. Catholic Charities USA is the nation's largest private network of social service organizations. One out of four AIDS patients in the world is in a health care facility run by the Catholic Church. So the Church is still flourishing in its life and its works.

One final statistic to think about. While Catholics constitute the largest religious group in the United States, the second largest denomination—ahead of the Southern Baptists—is former Catholics. Think what they might add to the life of the Church.

[45] See David DeLambo, "Executive Summary from the forthcoming survey, Lay Parish Ministers: A Study of Emerging Leadership," *Church* 21/3 (Fall 2005) 4–8.

[46] See USCCB, "Renewing Our Commitment to Catholic Elementary and Secondary Schools in the Third Millennium."

Index

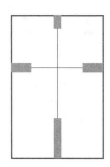

Abortion, 7, 88
Analogy of being, 27–28
Armstrong, Karen, 35
Atkinson, Joseph, 54, 56
Augustine, 113
Authority in the Church, 105–109,
    116, 118

Baigent, Michael, 38
Barron, Robert, 28–29, 32–33, 65
Barth, Karl, 28–29
Bauerschmidt, Frederick, 98
Beckwith, John, 25
Bellah, Robert, 9–10
Belting, Hans, 26
Benedict XVI, Pope, 19, 85, 96
Bock, Darrell, 37, 43, 44
Bourg, Florence, 55, 63
Brackley, Dean, 79
Brading, David, 33
Brown, Dan, 37
Buddhism, 23

Calvin, John, 10, 28, 30–32
Canon of the NT, 42–43
CARA, 6
Cardinal Newman Society, 75–76
Carroll, Colleen, 88
Catholic Church, 105–109
    and credibility problem, 15, 106,
        116

as unique, xiv, 90, 111–114
as voluntary society, xi, 12, 15, 118
leaving the, 7–9
Catholic colleges, universities, 66–86,
    117–118
    and "critical mass," 77
    FOCUS, 899
    neoconservative colleges, 66
    student life at, 83–85
    theology in, 71–75
Catholic identity, xi–xvi
    and art, 25–26, 32–33
    and mass attendance, 6, 90
    and new apologists, 109–111
    and social justice, 7
    and subculture, 13–15
    and young adults, xi, 1–19, 87–101,
        114–116
    characteristics of, xii–xv
Catholicism, Catholic, xii–xv
    as way of life, 14, 117
    Catholic imagination, xiv, 20–35,
        110
    Catholic Studies, 80–82
    Catholic theology, 29–35, 71–75
    immigrant style of, 14
    laity, 107–108, 118
    statistics on, 114, 119
    uniqueness of, 111–114
Cavadini, John, 16
Cesareo, Francesco, 80

Chauvet, Louis-M, xiii
Chesterton, G. K., 9
Christology, 40–41, 104
City of the Angels Film Festival, 33
Coleman, John, 2, 115
Communion, xiii, 113, 114
Constantine, Emperor, 39–43
Converts and reverts, 99–100
Crossan, John, 42–43
Cushman, Robert, 29

D'Antonio, William, 92, 106
Davidson, James, xi, 3, 4, 16, 86, 87, 90, 111
Da Vinci Code, 36–50
Day, Dorothy, 112
Deism, Moralistic, 11, 18, 117
DeLambo, David, 119
Docetism, 47
Domestic church, 51–65
    in documents, 53–54
Duffy, Eamon, 32
Dulles, Avery, 29

Eberstadt, Mary, 55
Eckhard, Meister, 27
Ecumenism, 110–111
Ehrman, Bart, 39
Eire, Carlos, 31, 32
Ellacuría, Ignatio, 79
Ellis, John T., 13–14
Ellsberg, Robert, 59–60
Epp, Eldon, 45
Evangelical Catholics, 89–91
Evangelicals, 8, 12, 33–34, 37, 82, 100
Evangelization, 12, 90, 95, 111
Ex Corde Ecclesiae, 69–71

Fahey, Michael, 73
Faulkner, Tom, 38
Fellowship of Catholic University Students (FOCUS), 89
Fisher, James, 81
Flanagan, Caitlin, 84

Fournier, Keith, 89
Francis, Mark, 108
Francis of Assisi, 26, 59
Froehle, Bryan, 6

Gaillardetz, Richard, 4–5, 13, 107, 110–111, 112
Gallagher, Michael, 17
Gallin, Alice, 67
Gautier, Mary, 6
Gelpi, Albert, 80
Gilkey, Langdon, 26
Gnostic gospels, 41–43
Gnosticism, 43–47
God, 23–24, 27–31
Grabar, André, 25
Greeley, Andrew, xiv, 15, 20, 25, 28, 32, 57, 81–82, 109, 116
Grodi, Marcus, 100
Groome, Thomas, 55–56, 61
Gunton, Colin, 28
Guroian, Vigen, 84

Hadaway, C., 2
Hahn, Scott, 96–97, 100
Haight, Roger, 40, 109
Hatcher, Robert, 83
Haug, Werner and Phillipe Warner, 58
Haughey, John, 12, 67, 74, 90
Hays, Edward, 60
Hellwig, Monika, 17, 74, 95
Hispanic Catholics, 7–8, 62
Hoge, Dean, xi, 3, 4, 16, 52, 87, 90, 105–106, 111, 115–116, 118
Homosexuality, 7, 88
Howard, Thomas, 96–97, 100
Hurtado, Larry, 40

Iconoclasm, 32
Ignatius of Loyola, 26–27
Individualism, religious, xiii, 9–11, 102–105
Islam, 23, 32

Jenkins, Philip, 42
Jesus, 27, 45–47
John Damascene, 26
John of the Cross, 27
John Paul II, Pope, 12, 69, 93, 97
Judaism, 24, 32

Kaplan, Grant, 99
Kasper, Walter, 107, 113
Kaveny, Cathleen, 16
Keating, Karl, 91, 96–97, 109
Klimoski, Victor, 94
Koessler, John, 21
Kreeft, Peter, 96–97, 100
Küng, Hans, 112–113

Land O'Lakes Statement, 67
Landy, Thomas, 80
Langan, John, 68, 77
Layton, Bentley, 42, 44
Luther, Martin, 28, 31

Madrid, Patrick, 97, 109
Mandatum, 71, 73
Marler, Penny, 2
Marsden, George, 68–69
Mary Magdalene, 45–47, 49
Mary, Marian devotion, 21–22, 29,
    32, 61
McBrien, Richard, xii
McDonnell, Kilian, 104–105, 107
McGuire, Meredith, 10
McKnight, Scot, 100
Mediation, xiii, 10, 24
Meier, John, 43
Merton, Thomas, 27
Miller, J., 85
Miller, Robert, 42
Modras, Ronald, 49
Morris, Charles, 13–14

Nantais, David, 99
National Catholic Reporter Survey, 4, 85

Nature and grace, xiii, 30–31
New apologists, 96–97, 100, 109–111
Newman, John Henry, 79
Nicaea, Council of, 39–41
Nietzsche, Friedrich, 104
Nolan, Mary, 21
Noll, Mark, 100
Notre Dame Study, 3

Oakley, Francis and Bruce Russett, 198
O'Brien, David, 14, 89
O'Collins, Gerald, 41
O'Dea, Thomas, 14
Olson, Carl and Sandra Miesel, 38,
    44, 49
Osborne, Joan, 50
O'Toole, James, 14
Our Lady of Guadalupe, 33

Pabble, Martin, 12
Pagels, Elaine, 39, 43, 44
Parishes, 118
Passon, Richard, 77
Picknett, Lynn, 38
Poorman, Mark, 16
Pope, Stephen, 79
Portier, William, 13–15, 69, 89–91, 111
Power, David, 25
Priory of Sion, 38
Protestant theology, imagination,
    21–22, 27–35

Quinn, John, 106–107

Rahner, Karl, 21, 56, 63
Rausch, Thomas, xv, 41, 97, 108, 109,
    114
Reformation theology, xiii, 27–35
Robertson, Roland, 114
Rohr, Richard, 62
Roof, Wade, 10
Ruddy, Christopher, 98–99
Rudolph, Kurt, 44, 45

Sacraments, sacramentality, xiii, 26, 56–57, 63–64
Schreiter, Robert, 94
Schuth, Katarina, 91–93
Scorsese, Martin, 33
Search for Common Ground, 3
Self, as autonomous, 104–105
Seminarians, 17, 91–95
Shea, Mark, 97, 100
Sheila-ism, 10
Smith, Christian, 4, 11, 52, 64, 103, 114–115
Sobrino, Jon, 79
Society, Catholic and Protestant views of, 31
Spirituality, 1–2, 26–27, 102–103
    apophatic, 23, 27
    autonomous, 10, 102–105
    kataphatic, 23, 26
    "spiritual but not religious," 102–105
Starbird, Margaret, 39
Steinberg, Leo, 32, 49
Steinfels, Peter, 8, 68–69, 71, 72, 77, 78

Tertullian, 47
Thomas Aquinas, 27
Tracy, David, xiv, 20
Trier, Lars von, 33

UCLA Study, 1–2, 114
Universidad Centroamericana, 78–79
University of North Carolina Study, 4, 52, 114

Vagina Monologues, The, 76
Visions and Prophecies, 21–22
Vlazny, John, 76

Watson, William, 84
Whalen, David, 88–89
Wilcox, Brad, 55
Wilkes, Paul, 78
Williams, Andrea, 11
Wills, Garry, 14
Wister, Robert, 72
Witchcraft, 48–49
Witherington, Ben, 38, 45, 46, 50
Women in the Church, 2, 8, 37, 44–45
Wuthnow, Robert, 10, 35, 102–103

Yahweh, 40, 48
Young Catholics, 1–19, 87–101, 114–116
    and authority, 6–7, 106, 108, 116
    and evangelization, 12, 90, 95
    and mass attendance, 7, 90
    and parents, 52–53, 64, 85, 116–117
    and sexuality, 7, 83–84, 90, 106
    and social justice, 7
    as teenagers, 52, 114, 116
    as theologians, 96–99
    new generation, 87–101, 115–116
    theological illiteracy of, 16–18, 86, 89, 114–115

Zilbauer, Brian, 2